W9-BBU-434

An Institutional Investor Publication

State-of-the-Art
Portfolio
Selection

◆

Using Knowledge-Based Systems to Enhance Investment Performance

Robert R. Trippi
Jae K. Lee

PROBUS PUBLISHING COMPANY
Chicago, Illinois
Cambridge, England

© 1992 by Robert R. Trippi and Jae K. Lee

ISBN 1-55738-295-6

Printed in the United States of America

BC

1 2 3 4 5 6 7 8 9 0

Dedications

To my wife and best friend, Cecilia. R. R. T.

To my Lord, my students, and investors. J. K. L.

Contents at a Glance

v

Table of Contents

List of Figures

List of Tables

Preface

This book covers a broad spectrum of topics associated with the application of computerized knowledge-based systems, also called expert systems (ES), to investment decision making. As investing is an interesting and significant economic activity, and as powerful computers have in recent years become generally accessible, this subject is for us an exciting one.

As researchers and consultants, we became interested in writing a book on this subject several years ago. When we first became acquainted with ES, the technology was very new. We soon witnessed a shaking-out period that included the rapid acceptance and then abandonment of entire theoretical approaches and products based on them. As a result, a much more hardware- and software-independent view of knowledge-based systems now prevails in both industry and academia.

In undertaking this project, we wanted to focus on investment activities that could profit most from knowledge-based system deployment. Many of the earliest reported ES implementations, such as credit assessment and market monitoring, merely automated information-intensive or time-consuming tasks. As we gained experience with knowledge-based systems, it became clear that these systems had great potential for providing a significant performance edge in portfolio construction.

The audience for a book such as this appeared minuscule just a few years ago. Since then, however, reports from both industry and academia of successful deployments of knowledge-based systems have turned from a trickle into a flood; thus, we now feel confident that *State-of-the-Art Portfolio Selection* will find a receptive audience.

The major goals of this book are: (1) to inform readers about the potential benefits of knowledge-based systems in investment; (2) to examine design issues so as to enable readers to evaluate the philosophy and features of specific existing or proposed systems; and (3) to inspire the development of more advanced systems in the future.

This book is addressed to three audiences, the first being those, such as money managers, analysts, traders, and researchers, with portfolio decision-making or decision-support responsibilities. ES approaches described in this book can be applied to the portfolio operations of brokerage companies, investment management companies, mutual funds, insurance companies, pension funds, foundations, bank trust departments, and other institutions.

This book is addressed also to information-systems professionals who are either working in or are interested in learning about investment management systems. Although some in this group will already be familiar with the basics of ES construction, the unique character of the portfolio selection domain presented here will likely be new to most, as will the details of implementation such as designing portfolio optimization models to incorporate expert and manager inputs.

Finally, we hope to see this book used as a primary or supplemental text in graduate business courses. Most investment texts fail to discuss even rudimentary computer implementations of the economic theories and principles involved in investment management. The approaches to system building and real-life examples presented in this book should provide students with a clear idea of what they can expect to encounter upon entering industry.

The authors wish to thank the School of Business Administration at California State University, Long Beach, for its support in this endeavor; and in particular, to thank Dean Robert Deans for his encouragement, and professors Richard Harriff, Lawrence Sherman, and Hamdi Bilici for their helpful suggestions regarding various portions of the manuscript. Thanks also to Professor Suck Chin Chu at Kyunggi University, Dr. Hyun Soo Kim, Mr. Suhn Baum Kwon, Mr. Woo Ju Kim, and Mr. Ki Young Gwak, who together developed the K-FOLIO system while graduate students at the Decision Support and Expert Systems Laboratory of the Korea Advanced Institute of Science and Technology; to the Lucky Securities Company, especially its president, N. M. Hur, Dr. Suk-Ryong Lee, and Mr. Chung Chul Shin, who manages the K-FOLIO system known as BRAINS with the help of associates at Lucky and KAIST; and to Ms. Myung Wha Joung, who helped with the editing of the manuscript.

A portion of the royalties from this book will be used to further the study of Mr. Yang Soo Cho, a blind doctoral student who is studying at the University of Pittsburgh.

CHAPTER 1

Introduction

1.1   Knowledge-Based Systems and Investing
1.2   Organization of This Book

1.1   KNOWLEDGE-BASED SYSTEMS AND INVESTING

We are in the midst of a revolution in investment management. An unprecedented globalization of financial markets, advances in the electronic transmission of data, the accessibility of inexpensive yet extremely powerful computer hardware and software, and the migration during the past decade of so-called quants and computer wizards to Wall Street have all contributed to this revolution.

The body of finance theory and empirical evidence related to rational investment decision making has become so large that any future advances are expected to be incremental. Thus, the coming decades will likely bring a consolidation and accelerated application of this knowledge. Today, the keyword "apply" is virtually synonymous with "computerize."

The computerization of investment decision-making activities requires software systems that integrate mathematical models, a source of data, and a user interface. Such systems are generally referred to as *decision support systems,* or DSSs. That form of DSS whose database in-

1

cludes relevant theory, facts, and human knowledge and expertise is called a *knowledge-based system*, also referred to as an *intelligent* or *expert system* (ES).

The earliest expert systems were used in medicine, engineering, and the sciences. Although originally perceived as a niche area of artificial intelligence (AI), ES received considerable attention in both the academic and business press during the 1980s. Despite the sometimes excessive hype and optimism with which knowledge-based systems were first received, their most auspicious applications still lie in the future. ES technology holds great promise for enhancing a multitude of tasks performed in the financial services industries, and particularly in investment portfolio management activities.

The renewed interest in applying knowledge-based systems to business decisions can be attributed mostly to the plummeting costs of hardware and software. In the early 1980s, ES software and a suitable platform to run it on typically cost $100,000 or more. By the 1990s, equivalent or superior hardware–software systems could be had for under $5,000. Financial ES applications are now viewed as ideal proving grounds for new expert systems concepts and products, because in the realm of finance, significant, rapid, and easily measurable economic benefits can often be achieved.

Initially, expert systems were viewed as tools to enable nonexperts to make decisions as well as would one or more experts in a particular field, or *domain*. In fact, as will be discussed later in this book, ES technology is capable of achieving more *consistent* results, uncovering more knowledge, and reacting more quickly than would a group of humans. (Some ESs can respond in real time to a rapidly arriving data stream.)

How would an intelligent system function in the portfolio investment domain? Consider the problem of how to allocate a large sum of money among stocks, bonds, real estate, and precious metals. An ES used for this purpose would probably include the knowledge of several experts in each of these areas of investment in its database; such a database is called a *knowledge base*. A money manager using such a system could, in theory, manage a portfolio including several asset classes more effectively and at less cost, than could any of the individual domain experts whose knowledge is incorporated into the system. The most obvious advantages of integrating some form of computer intelligence into the portfolio decision-making process include permanence, usually a much lower cost, and a greater consistency of results in comparison to continually consulting with a team of experts.

While not every ES used to aid investment has been successful, it appears that most early failures stemmed from randomly applying AI technology rather than tailoring the system to a particular investment domain. Also, excessive attention has sometimes been given to emphasizing user friendliness in the form of natural language interfaces and graphic display facilities. The amounts spent on these niceties were amounts not available for improving the economic performance of the system. Fortunately, user friendliness can be achieved today at a much lower cost than it could even a few years ago.

1.2   THE ORGANIZATION OF THIS BOOK

Because it deals with the application of computers to investment management, *State-of-the-Art Portfolio Selection* can be thought of as a bridge between finance and information science. As such, it covers a broad spectrum of topics, using vocabulary drawn from both disciplines.

Chapter 2 deals in a general way with the investment environment and the characteristics of security markets. Market complexity and efficiency, determination of value, the nature of risk, and other issues of importance in the investment domain are discussed in this chapter. Although this book does not focus on the empirical evidence for market anomalies, knowledge-based systems are the most effective means available for recognizing and exploiting in a systematic fashion any anomalies that may exist.

Chapter 3 is a brief primer on portfolio theory. It contains a review of the concepts that are essential to understanding rational portfolio selection, with an emphasis on the Markowitz quadratic programming model. Also discussed in this chapter are the aggregate market implications of Markowitz portfolio optimization, including the Capital Asset Pricing Model. Knowledge-based systems' greatest potential lies in improving investment performance in a portfolio rather than single-asset framework.

Chapter 4 begins with an overview of knowledge-based systems. This includes a discussion of both conventionally implemented ES and knowledge-based systems built around neural networks. This chapter also contains a number of synopses of ES applications in the financial services industry. In each of these the goal is typically to improve risk/return performance in some sort of investment activity. Although this book is mainly concerned with portfolio selection, this chapter also describes systems capable of screening financial information, recognizing patterns in prices, and evaluating credit.

Chapter 5 discusses problem solving in general, and outlines the basic elements common to most expert systems. Also introduced are concepts of knowledge representation and inference relevant to the investment domain. (These will be examined in greater detail in later chapters.) This chapter also discusses the ways in which portfolio management systems can be tailored not only to the selection of stocks and industries, but also to timing and allocation decisions. In addition, we show how knowledge-based systems can provide reasons for their decisions in a form that can be understood by investors (a feat that most traditional quantitative approaches, such as time series models, cannot perform).

Using illustrative examples, Chapter 6 focuses on both the representation of knowledge as rules and the types of rules most pertinent to the investment domain. Issues associated with the construction of synergistic rule bases are discussed, including strategies for resolving conflicts, developing explanations from the rule base, and the sorts of user dialogue possible with respect to individual securities and industries or sectors.

Chapter 7 deals with handling uncertainty, a topic that is especially germane to the building of knowledge-based portfolio selection systems. Several approaches to inference under uncertainty are described, including the Bayesian, certainty factor, and fuzzy-logic approaches.

Chapter 8 covers topics related to knowledge acquisition, integration, and maintenance. These topics include representational adequacy; the collectability (whether from human experts or from machine learning systems) and maintainability of relevant knowledge; aids for dynamic knowledge maintenance; and the integration with expert knowledge of investor knowledge, assumptions, and preferences.

Chapter 9 discusses the role of machine learning in the context of portfolio selection and revision. Acquisition and maintenance of knowledge is a bottleneck of most existing expert systems. Due to the difficulty of acquiring and validating knowledge from humans in a timely manner, extensive application of machine learning is a virtual necessity for successful systems in the investment domain. Topics covered include inductive and pattern-based syntactic learning, the use of genetic algorithms for rule-set generation, and a review of neural networks used to predict the performance of companies and securities.

Chapter 10 discusses mechanisms for incorporating the Markowitz portfolio optimization model into a knowledge-based system. It is shown how the model can be augmented with constraints derived from rules, and how the quadratic programming algorithm can be extended to a multistep sequential algorithm that considers the priority of decision variables. Interpreting up-to-date knowledge in conjunction with optimization represents a crucial technology for portfolio decision making.

Chapter 11 introduces database and knowledge-base terminology, outlines the evolution of database technologies relevant to expert system construction, and discusses methods for interfacing expert systems with conventional investment information systems. This chapter will also outline the major issues associated with managing fundamental and price and volume data, and introduce the concept of a function base (one that permits expansion of available data items without adding to the storage burden).

Chapter 12 illustrates the concepts discussed in previous chapters by describing a session in which the K-FOLIO system is used. During this session, environmental assumptions are selected, stocks and industries are evaluated, and a portfolio is constructed by applying knowledge and investor preferences to the modified Markowitz model of Chapter 10.

Chapter 13 is a summary of conclusions concerning the design of systems for maximum effectiveness in portfolio decision making, and suggests several promising areas for further research.

CHAPTER 2

Nature of the Security Investment Domain

2.1   CHARACTERISTICS OF INVESTMENT ASSETS[1]

Investment assets can be real (physical) or financial. Factories, farmland, and buildings are real assets. Financial assets include contractual commitments of future payment such as commercial paper and debentures; and claims on assets such as cash, stocks, options, and commodity and currency futures contracts. Securities are formal instruments that represent ownership of financial assets and facilitate their trade; the process of creating securities from assets is called *securitization*. This book deals mainly with investment in financial assets. Buyers of these assets must take into account factors such as *liquidity, size of the trading unit, transaction costs, leverage potential*, and *pattern of returns over time*.

Liquidity is characteristic of assets that can be bought and sold in any quantity without their price changing significantly; liquidity indirectly represents the average trade size as a fraction of total trading volume, and often impacts spreads between bid and ask prices. Proposed measures of liquidity include the ratio of dollar volume of trading to the absolute percentage change in the price of completed transactions (e.g., see Cooper, Groth, and Avera 1985) and the average absolute value of trade-to-trade percentage price change divided by the number of transactions (Marsh and Rock 1986). Liquidity is important not only because it facilitates trading, but also because prices may convey little or no information about an asset's value if the asset does not have at least a minimal level of liquidity. In the hierarchy of asset liquidity, value is most meaningfully represented by prices derived from actively traded organized markets, and least meaningfully by prices derived from sparsely traded and unorganized markets.

Financial assets vary considerably in trading unit size. These units may cost a few hundred dollars, as in the case of low-priced exchange-listed stocks and stock options; or tens or hundreds of thousands of dollars, as in the case of certain mortgage-backed debt instruments and futures contracts. Securities such as Treasury bills, notes and bonds, and common and preferred stock of large corporations are usually tradable in units (shares or lots) that are of moderate size as well as highly liquid.

Commissions for most financial assets, relative to the dollar size of the trade, are generally in the low single digits, and decline with the size of the transaction. The structure of transaction costs varies greatly; for example, bid-ask spreads are generally much greater than commissions for commodity futures, but less than commissions for most options. Transaction costs can effectively constrain the types of investment strategies that can be practically employed. Since total transaction costs are relatively low for futures contracts, investing strategies involving purchase and sale on the same day do not result in much loss of capital to commissions. In contrast, real estate is almost always a multiyear investment because of the high costs involved in doing any transaction. These costs include not only commissions, but also legal and title costs, loan fees, and the managerial attention required to effect a purchase or sale.

Transaction costs may be *symmetrical* or *asymmetrical*. Real estate transaction costs are highly asymmetrical, favoring the purchase. Commissions, figured as a percentage of the gross sale price, are normally paid only by the seller. In contrast, the transaction costs of front-load mutual funds are also asymmetrical but favor the sale. In other words, the purchase of shares involves greater fees than their eventual sale.

Leverage potential refers to the proportion of cash that must be committed at the time of purchase. Most investment assets can be bought using leverage, with loaned funds collateralized by the asset. The leverage potential of securities varies considerably, according to *margin requirements* set by exchanges and regulatory agencies. For example, at present, the margin requirements for futures contracts are much lower than those for most other securities.

The possibility of receiving returns is the prime motivation for owning investment assets. Returns can take the form of price appreciation, periodic monetary payments (for example, rent, interest, and dividends), or both. The precise pattern of returns is significant in investment theory and practice, and statistical parameters such as mathematical expectation, variance, skewness, and distribution of returns over time often figure prominently in the characterization of assets.

2.2. THEORIES OF STOCK PRICE DETERMINATION

Investment theory and practice is an evolving branch of economic science. Since the pioneering work of John Burr Williams (1936) and Graham and Dodd (1934), the valuation of capital stock and other types of securities has been a source of intense interest and constant debate among investors, academicians, and individuals and institutions concerned with wealth. Formidable intellectual resources have been directed toward achieving the goal of buying low and selling high.

2.2.1   Random, Ordered, and Complex Systems

Dynamic systems may be classified according to this degree of orderliness. *Random systems* are totally chaotic, while *ordered systems* operate predictably according to reliable mathematical rules, such as those of physics and chemistry. *Complex systems* possess characteristics of both ordered and random systems. There is much evidence that stock markets behave as complex systems (Jacobs and Levy 1989).

The stochastic processes that govern nonordered systems may be *stationary* or *nonstationary*. The processes that drive stock markets exhibit a considerable degree of nonstationarity. Forecasting relevant parameters is far more difficult in nonstationary than in stationary systems.

2.2.2   Value-Based Investing

Early theories of stock price determination viewed markets as ordered systems. It seemed logical that the value of an asset should equal the discounted value of its stream of payments or returns, whether in the form of dividends, interest, or earnings. Thus, it was considered desirable to identify factors that impact the return stream, for such knowledge would also confer on its possessor knowledge of whether the asset is currently under- or overpriced in the market relative to its intrinsic value. The *dividend discount model* (DDM), introduced by Williams (1936) is one of the earliest *value-based investing* approaches. Value-based investing later focused primarily on corporate earnings, accepting Miller and Modigliani's (1961) arguments that the value of the firm should be relatively unaffected by the dividend payout ratio.

One standard approach to security analysis is the methodology known as *fundamental analysis*. In this approach to valuing assets (which received considerable attention in universities in the 1960s and 1970s and is still popular today), the market is viewed as a relatively ordered system and each company is represented by characteristics such as financial ratios and performance measures, which are used to draw inferences about that company.

Accounting ratios that are given substantial emphasis in fundamental analysis include price-to-earnings (P/E), price-to-cash flow, market value-to-book value per share, sales-to-price and yield, current ratios, debt ratios, and those based on leverage factors, sales forecasts, and projected earnings. More recent measures of interest include beta coefficient and variance or standard deviation of earnings (see Chapter 3).

Such measures may be worthy of examination in their own right, but different financial analysts will often reach different conclusions regarding the likely impact of such characteristics on future earnings and/or dividends. As a foundation for value-based investing, fundamental analysis suffers from the fact that, as empirical research has shown, stock prices and discounted dividend streams are generally not very closely correlated (see Jacobs and Levy 1988). By the 1970s, fundamental analysis was considered by leading academicians to be a somewhat simplistic approach to value-based investing.

2.2.3   The Efficient Market Hypothesis

In the 1960s, as the field of finance became more scientific, the theory building and testing that followed became based more closely on economic theory, making market efficiency a major issue. The *efficient market hypothesis* (EMH) and the *capital asset pricing model* (see Chapter 3) were consistent with numerous previous studies that found stock-price fluctuations to be random (several of the early studies can be found in Cootner 1964). According to the EMH, the pattern of past prices provides little or no indication as to the direction of future prices.

The essence of the EMH is that at any point in time, prices of securities in an efficient market already reflect the assimilation of all information available to participants in the markets. Several different forms of the EMH were proposed, each dealing with a different type of information. The *weak form* considers past price information only, the *semistrong form* considers all publicly available information, and the *strong form* considers all information publicly and privately available. The weak form implies that prices follow a *random walk* in which successive changes in price have zero correlation.

The weak and semistrong forms were fairly well supported with respect to stock and other security markets in a number of research studies. The strong form is difficult to prove or disprove, since profiting from information withheld from the public is an illegal activity in the United States and in most other countries with organized exchanges.

Studies examining publicly disclosed insider trading have generally concluded that insider trades result in higher-than-average returns. Many studies of the strong form of the EMH have focused on the performance of mutual-fund managers under the assumption that these individuals may in the course of their business come into nonpublic information. Generally, these studies have not found fund managers to be superior to other investor types, although there is some evidence that a small group of managers could possess superior knowledge and skills (Lee and Rahman 1991). Synopses of early empirical studies defending the EMH can be found in Lorie et al. (1975), and a lucid nontechnical treatment of the subject appears in Malkiel (1990).

By the mid-1970s, most finance theorists conceded that the organized markets for stocks and other securities were for the most part efficient, and that proprietary techniques of stock selection would not result in performance consistently superior to that of broad-based market indexes. In fact, choosing portfolios by throwing darts at the stock market listings was proposed by more than one academician interested in promoting the EMH. Still, while the EMH was not easy to refute, neither was it easy to prove beyond a shadow of a doubt. Some research did produce results that, although perhaps inconsistent with parts of the EMH, did not contradict its fundamental assumptions. For example, Fama (1963,1965) found that the changes in the prices of stocks were distributed more in accordance with the stable Paretian than the more restrictive Normal distribution predicted by the random walk theory.

The stock market's equivalent of dart throwing was the passive management of investment funds. Under this strategy, a portfolio representative of the market or a segment of the market is selected and managed using a buy-and-hold strategy, with the only decision making being related to the exclusion of extreme investments. From the late 1970s to the present, index funds have proliferated, which shows investors' faith in the EMH as well as their acceptance of security markets as random systems.

2.2.4.   Beyond the EMH

The EMH does not support the *technical analysis* approach to investing, that is, predicting future stock prices by using both historical price and volume data and *indicators,* such as leading indexes and market-derived statistical measures. One popular form of technical analysis is *charting*, in which graphic displays of past price performance, moving- average trends, cycles, and intra- or inter-day stock price ranges are studied in an attempt to discern cues for profitable trading. Charting, especially when applied to commodity futures trading, makes use of techniques such as moving indexes, trend analysis, turning-point indicators, cyclical spectral analysis, and the recognition of various formations or patterns in prices (with these patterns being assigned names such as "flags," "triangles," and "head-and-shoulders"), in order to forecast subsequent price behavior.

Efficient market theory, supported by most academic studies of technical analysis, contradicts the notion that patterns in the price and volume of securities can alone provide any significant advantage in predicting future price movements. In fact, many individuals who have promoted new technical analysis methodologies have earned more by writing books and newsletters based on their creations than they ever did by investing, and services selling technical charts have flourished.

Insights drawn from the EMH framework have been of immense help to those who study the behavior of stock-market prices and aggregate market behavior. Nevertheless, because security markets are complex, time-variant (nonstationary), and probably nonlinear dynamic systems, noncomplex theories cannot adequately represent their behavior; thus, it is not surprising that naive technical rules are ineffective in exploiting whatever inefficiencies may exist.

In the 1980s, there was both a resurgence of interest in questions of efficiency and a variety of empirical tests developed of new and often elaborate theories that sought to explain subtle security-pricing regularities and other anomalies. Although an earlier study by King (1966) did find an economy effect, an industry effect, and a security effect associated with stock-price changes, the effects were not consistent for each stock studied. Rather, they varied with each particular company and its unique characteristics.

More recently, there have been attempts to isolate or "purify" individual factors associated with apparent return anomalies, the aim being to expose the factors that are just proxies for other factors, and identify factors that affect returns only when present in tandem. In a regression study in 1988, Jacobs and Levy found that the following pure effects were statistically significant at the one percent level: low P/E ratio, small size (capitalization), ratio of sales to stock price, trend in analysts' forecast of earnings (with one-, two-, and three-month lag), earnings surprise (one-month lag), relative strength, and one- and two-month residual reversals. Although the January seasonal effect was in general strong for P/E effect, it was insignificant for firm size. *Multidimensional screens* can be used to identify individual stocks exhibiting such convoluted pricing anomalies.

Findings like the preceding suggest that the EMH is not a perfect representation of the realities of markets that behave as complex systems. Moreover, with the growth of large institutional investors, by the 1990s there was widespread suspicion that the behavior of stock markets was becoming more irrational in some respects, as small minority interests often mixed with larger sales, and could in some cases even block and control positions. On the one hand, the evolution of markets dominated by institutional investors using computer-driven program trading systems appeared to be resulting in more anomalies. On the other hand, the level of technological sophistication applied to recognizing and exploiting pockets of market inefficiency, and ultimately eliminating them, was also increasing (Keane 1991).

2.3   RISK ISSUES

2.3.1   What Is Risk?

Risk means different things to different market participants. For theory-building, it is important that risk be defined in terms of rational investors, and it is desirable (though not essential) that there is a consensus among all rational investors as to what constitutes risk. Investors are normally assumed to be averse to risk. In the standard capital asset pricing model, risk is defined in terms of either the deviations of returns from a market index or standard deviation or variance of returns. This is essentially a behavioral assumption. If behaviorally accurate, models of rational investment that consider probability of loss, mean absolute deviation of returns, or semivariance of returns[2] as the cardinal measure of risk could be just as valid. Moreover, if fundamental measures such as current yield, P/E relationships, trading volume, and cash-flow considerations have different meanings to different investor classes, the same would probably be true of any specific measure of risk.

The study of the psychology of investors is still in its infancy. The economic theory upon which the capital asset pricing model rests assumes that investors will have a rational response to risk and return known as *utility maximization*. In general, realistic models of rational decision making under this framework must take into account different utility or response functions for different investors or investor classes.

2.3.2   Cognitive Error and Stochastic Risk Modeling

As will be seen in Chapter 3, there is generally a positive, although sometimes less than perfect, relationship between investment risk and return. There can also exist substantial error in connection with the assessment of risk. Risk is a function of both company operations, reflected by fundamentals, and the market's interpretation of that information, which is subject to errors of cognition. For this reason the price of a small firm's stock can fluctuate by 10% or more in a single day, although there may have been no change in the firm's profitability, products, or management. In order to model actual risk accurately, one must take into account the contribution of cognitive error to apparent risk.

2.4   MARKET PSYCHOLOGY AND NOISE

In an attempt to ascribe rationality to market participants, technical analysis often attributes past security price patterns to market psychology. However, it is not past prices, but future prices or expectations of future prices that are of concern to most investors (Schmalensee 1976). In studying the predictive content of prices, industry effects, and market effects, errors are bound to occur because of the uncertain environment and the multiplicity of factors that are subject to different interpretations by market participants. Even insiders sometimes make wrong investment decisions.

The "Black Monday" market crash of October 19, 1987 illustrates that although aggregate mispricing due to faulty perceptions about intrinsic value may persist, eventually adjustments to value considerations do take place. It is usually maintained by those who attribute aggregate price cycles to investor psychology that "bull" markets reflect periods of general optimism and "bear" markets reflect periods of general pessimism.

The loss of principal may have differing psychological effects on different investors, resulting in specific securities over- or underreacting to news items (also called transient over- and undershoot). Strategies that seek to exploit mispricing transients are called *noise-trading* strategies. Successful noise trading requires the rapid detection of short-persistence deviations of prices from intrinsic values.

2.5   INSTITUTIONAL TRADING AND MARKET BEHAVIOR

2.5.1   Agency and Database Commonality Effects

Problems of *agency* make institutional trading somewhat different from other trading. The professional money manager may be punished or fired for poor performance. In such a situation, there is a tendency to gravitate toward investment strategies, such as *portfolio insurance*, that minimize the probability of losses (Perold and Sharpe 1988). Portfolio insurance is a *convex dynamic* investment strategy requiring almost continuous adjustment of risky and risk-free asset proportions (discontinuous adjustment is discussed in Trippi and Harriff 1990). Such strategies produce return distributions with shortened or truncated downside tails (positive skewness) and diminished mathematical expectation relative to a buy-and-hold strategy of identical standard deviation risk. Salaried managers may find such strategies appealing because, having one employer, they cannot diversify away their personal income risk. However, at least in the case of public mutual funds, investor clients can diversify away fund-specific risk or at least moderate such risk by allocating a portion of their capital to riskless interest-paying assets. These clients would thus likely prefer that fund returns have symmetrical distributions with greater expected returns.

In the investment community, there are few information sources that are not available to all participants. Information is often obtained from similar or identical sources and analyzed using similar techniques. Therefore there is a tendency for funds dealing in similar asset classes to include similar specific assets. The institutional trader is concerned with short-term fluctuations, but generally has a long-term objective. If the fund's goal is simply to outperform a market index, it follows that a static investment mix with only minor variations from that particular index would be attractive since it minimizes transaction costs and eliminates the cost of an active portfolio manager.

2.5.2   Trading Dynamics and Instability

If a significant proportion of the trading in a market is driven by convex investment strategies, the market's volatility will increase, and returns of buy-and-hold participants in that market will become positively skewed, with longer downside than upside tail.

Various authors suggest that this and other types of institutional trading have contributed to an increase in intraday price volatility and that the proliferation of program trading systems may be a cause of instability. When the market is highly stressed, trading may be halted through the use of regulatory *circuit breakers*, which shut down trading when aggregate price movements and/or volumes exceed certain limits, eventually returning the market to a stable condition.

Institutional investors, especially when trading electronically, pay lower commissions than do individual investors. Thus, institutional investors have an incentive to act on minor market imperfections or transient price disequilibria, although less favorable order execution prices resulting from high intraday volatility may easily negate commission savings (Schwartz 1990).

2.6   THE EXPLOITATION OF ANOMALIES

2.6.1   The Cost and Value of Information

One measure of market efficiency is the way in which the market responds to information that enters it. The phenomenon, mentioned earlier, of over- and underreaction to the arrival of new information has been extensively studied. Ex post evidence of correcting reversals shows up as lagged negative serial correlation in price series (e.g., see DeBondt and Thaler 1987). Efficiency is a question of degree. If the market exhibits overshoot tendencies, for example, it is important to know in advance whether there is likely to be a net positive gain from acting on such inefficiencies. When transaction costs are substantial, even significant pockets of market inefficiency may be difficult to exploit profitably.

The costs and value of information are important in the context of portfolio construction. As will be discussed in Chapter 3, additional information makes it possible to revise one's assessments of risk and return of various securities, and thus combine those securities in more effective proportions. One measure of the value of information is the increase in expected return obtainable from reoptimizing the portfolio while maintaining the same level of risk. The additional knowledge is worth acquiring only if its cost is less than the difference in expected returns of the original and revised portfolios.

2.6.2   Implied Probability Distributions

Although those who use naive methods of technical analysis such as charting are rarely successful in predicting price movements, it is nonetheless possible for price and volume data to have predictive content of a qualitative nature. A form of knowledge that can be partially derived from historical trading data is the implied probability distribution of potential sellers' security costs.

Consider the following observations of trading activity for hypothetical securities A and B, which have identical price histories but different volume histories:

Time period	−5	−4	−3	−2	−1	Current
A Price	$10	9	9	11	11	$10
A Volume	100	75	75	125	125	
B Price	$10	9	9	11	11	$10
B Volume	100	125	125	75	75	

Let us assume first that the 500 shares above represent the total amount of trading done in these securities since they were first offered; second, that none of the traded shares are resales; and third, that the remaining shares are owned by long-term investors who are not at present interested in liquidation. From the above information one can infer the following table of probabilities associated with potential sellers' share acquisition prices:

Price	9	10	11
Security A	.3	.2	.5
Security B	.5	.2	.3

Suppose that this is the beginning of the last trading day in December and that of the shareholders who have taken losses (i.e., paid more than $10 per share), 40% have historically sold their shares on the last tax sale day. If, on the average, 10% of other shareholders turn over securities every day, then from the table of implied probabilities, it can be seen that the number of shares of Security A supplied today at a $10 price will be 500(.5)(.4), or 100, but that the number of shares of Security B supplied at $10 will be only 500(.3)(.4), or 60. In fact, it is possible to calculate the number of securities offered at every price, in effect constructing supply curves for these two securities before the market has even opened. Even were the securities to have identical intrinsic values, in the absence of information about demand it would be reasonable to expect that the market-clearing price of Security A today will be less than that of B.

Because securities are accumulated in a more-or-less continuous fashion over time, some portion of a given period's volume reflects the unwinding of positions already counted in previous periods' volume. Therefore, the implied probability model is incomplete, and can never provide exact share-cost probabilities. Nonetheless, if these assumptions about the actively traded pool of shares and the stochastic processes governing share accumulation and liquidation (such as these processes being Poisson) are valid, and if one goes far enough back in time, it should be possible to develop *bounds* on the share-cost probabilities implied by price and volume data for individual stocks. From time to time there may arise anomalies in such probability bounds (relative to some norm) that are exploitable. This is the theoretical underpinning for certain machine learning schemes employing price and volume data (see Chapter 9).

2.6.3   Decision Rules and Black-Box Investing

Since the turn of the century, investors have developed decision rules for recognizing and acting upon promising investment opportunities. Some classes of rules are static; that is, they are parameterized using information from one period. Others are adaptive; that is, they are based on knowledge of all past information and evolve over time. Investors may believe in the predictive validity of parsimonious or naive rules either because they have had past success with these rules or because they view the market as essentially noncomplex.

In recent years, theorists have developed numerous clever and complicated systems of decision rules, each of which, it is claimed, can beat the market. Some of these systems are entirely computer automated, while others require human intervention at one or more stages. Proprietary systems that require little or no human judgment are called *black boxes*. Only occasionally has the robustness of the mathematical rules programmed into black boxes been rigorously analyzed by researchers (e.g., see Trippi and Harriff 1989). The systems most likely to be successful are those that consider the full spectrum of security, industry, market, and exogenous economic factors within the framework of portfolio optimization, and that incorporate the knowledge and skills of experts. The theory and architecture of these systems, referred to as *knowledge-based systems*, will be discussed in later chapters of this book.

2.7   CONCLUSIONS

It can be argued that the consistently superior performance of some investors and investment experts is *prima facie* evidence that, although organized markets for stocks and other securities are for the most part efficient, pockets of inefficiency that result in irrational pricing arise at least occasionally. The fact that active management and passive management philosophies successfully coexist is a reflection of the widely divergent views on this subject in the financial community.

Market complexity is manifested in anomalous pricing (i.e., deviations of price from some measure of intrinsic or equilibrium value). Anomalies may arise from the market's incomplete assimilation of all available information about particular securities, lack of attention by market participants, differences of opinion about the meaning and significance of available data, response inertia, methodological flaws in valuation, or investors' inability to disentangle complex relationships within large data sets. When security markets are complex, the investment approaches most likely to produce exceptional results are those that synergistically combine multidimensional, nonlinear, and adaptive value-based decision-making rules. Such rules can be stored, maintained, and updated in a special form of database called a knowledge base.

ENDNOTES

1.   Thanks to Dr. Lawrence Sherman for his helpful contribution to this chapter.

2.   Semivariance is defined as

$$(1/n) \sum_{(i/r_i \leq \bar{r})} (r_i - \bar{r})^2$$

where r_i is the ith return observation and $\bar{r}$ is mean return. If returns are symmetrically distributed, semivariance is identical to half the variance.

REFERENCES

Cooper, S. K., Groth, J. C., and Avera, W. E., 1985. "Liquidity, Exchange Listing, and Common Stock Performance." *Journal of Economics and Business* (February): 21–33.

Cootner, P., ed., 1964. *The Random Character of Stock Market Prices.* Cambridge, Mass.: MIT Press.

DeBondt, W., and Thaler, R., 1987. "Further Evidence on Investor Overreaction and Stock Market Seasonality." *The Journal of Finance* 42, 3 (July):557–81.

Fama, E., 1963. "Mandelbrot and the Stable Paretian Hypothesis." *Journal of Business* 36, 4 (October): 420.

Fama, E., 1965. "The Behavior of Stock Market Prices." *Journal of Business* 38 (January): 35–105.

Graham, B., and Dodd, D., 1934. *Security Analysis.* New York: McGraw-Hill.

Jacobs, B., and Levy, K., 1989. "The Complexity of the Stock Market." *The Journal of Portfolio Management* 16, 1 (Fall): 19–27.

Jacobs, B., and Levy, K., 1988. "Disentangling Equity Return Irregularities: New Insights and Investment Opportunities." *Financial Analysts Journal* 44, 3 (May–June): 18–43.

Jacobs, B., and Levy, K. 1988. "On the Value of 'Value.'" *Financial Analysts Journal* 44, 4 (July–August): 47–62.

Keane, S. 1991., "Paradox in the Current Crisis in Efficient Market Theory." *The Journal of Portfolio Management* 17, 2 (Winter): 30–4.

King, B., 1966. "Market and Industry Factors in Stock Price Behavior." *Journal of Business* 39, 1 (January): 139–50.

Lee, C. F., and Rahman, S., 1991. "New Evidence on Timing and Security Selection Skill of Mutual Fund Managers." *The Journal of Portfolio Management* 17, 2 (Winter): 80–3.

Lorie, J., Dodd, P., and Kimpton, M., 1985. *The Stock Market: Theories and Evidence.* Homewood, Ill.: Dow-Jones Irwin Publishing Co.

Malkiel, B., 1990. *A Random Walk Down Wall Street.* New York: W. W. Norton Co.

Marsh, T., and Rock, K., 1986. "Exchange Listing and Liquidity: A Comparison of the American Stock Exchange with the NASDAQ National Market System." American Stock Exchange Transactions Data Research Project Report No. 2 (January).

Miller, M., and Modigliani, F., 1961. "Dividend Policy, Growth, and the Valuation of Shares." *Journal of Business* 34 (October): 411–33.

Perold, A. F., and Sharpe, W. F., 1988. "Dynamic Strategies for Asset Allocation." *Financial Analysts Journal* 44 (January–February): 16–27.

Schmalensee, R., 1976. "An Experimental Study of Expectation Formation." *Econometrica* 44, 1 (January): 17–41.

Trippi, R. R., and Harriff, R. B., "Performance of Portfolio Insurance with Discrete Rebalance Filter and Serially Correlated Prices." F. Fabozzi, ed., 1990. *Advances in Futures and Options Research.* Greenwich: JAI Press, 177–90.

Trippi, R. R., and Harriff, R. B., 1989. "Evaluation of the 'AIM' Dynamic Asset Allocation Strategy." *Southwest Journal of Business and Economics* 6 (Fall): 14–20.

Williams, J. B., 1936. *The Theory of Investment Value.* Cambridge, Mass.: Harvard University Press.

CHAPTER 3

Modern Approaches to Portfolio Selection

3.1 INTRODUCTION

In order to study knowledge-based systems approaches to portfolio selection, it is necessary to know something about the theory underlying

23

the construction of portfolios. As discussed in Chapter 2, investment management strategies involve both *timing* and *selection*. Possessing superior knowledge about individual securities could in principle enable an investor to allocate wealth in such a way as to realize greater returns and/or lower risk over time than other investors. Knowing the future direction of the stock market as a whole could also enable investors in a particular security or collection of securities to time their purchases and sales so as to reap abnormally high returns.

There are several popular approaches to making decisions regarding portfolio selection or wealth allocation. The simplest, the *conformance* approach, requires that portfolios be constructed with the goal of meeting the specific requirements of the investing institution or entity. Generally, the investor will want to hold fixed proportions of wealth in differing broad classes of assets, such as short- and long-term debt, equity, and foreign securities; and within each class, in securities representing certain industries, geographical locations, or "quality" groupings. Quality assessments may be based on company capitalization, performance history, or other organizations investing in that security. The earliest knowledge-based portfolio selection systems, such as that of Clarkson (described in the next chapter), employed conformance-allocation rules.

A strategy in which the asset mix is responsive to the state of the national or global economy (e.g., phases of the business cycle), is referred to as *tactical asset allocation*. Tactical asset allocation is often *contrarian*, shifting wealth into those assets that have suffered recent declines in value. When the proportions of wealth allocated to various asset classes or individual securities are revised in an anticipatory fashion, based on a specific set of forecasts of such macroeconomic factors as real economic growth, real interest rates, inflation rate, oil prices, and defense spending, the strategy is referred to as *scenario allocation*.

In tactical and scenario allocation, it is not uncommon to determine the desired asset mix by using regression or other quantitative techniques. If assets are viewed as possessing several relevant attributes, and desired mixes are specified in each attribute dimension, it is possible that there will exist no feasible combination of assets that satisfies all mix requirements. Although this problem may be resolved heuristically, the final mix is likely to be somewhat subjective.

A more objective portfolio selection paradigm is that of *optimization*, in which wealth is allocated across securities in such a way as to maximize or minimize some explicit criterion of success, subject to various constraints. Usually there are two or more success criteria that are in contention with one another. Two examples of optimization are *goal programming* and *mean-variance optimization.*

3.2   GOAL PROGRAMMING

In the goal programming approach to asset allocation, the quality of a portfolio is gauged by how close it comes to achieving target values or goals for each of several attributes. A collective measure of the magnitude of positive and negative deviations from attribute goals is used to evaluate the portfolio (e.g., see Ignizio 1976). Portfolio selection using this approach is represented by the following optimization problem:

$$\text{Minimize} \atop X \qquad D_p = \sum_{j=1}^{m} P_j^+ d_j^+ + \sum_{j=1}^{m} P_j^- d_j^-$$

subject to

$$\sum_{i=1}^{n} x_i C_{ij} + d_j^+ - d_j^- = G_j, \qquad j = 1, \ldots m$$

$$\sum_{i=1}^{n} x_i C_{ij} \geq L_j, \qquad j = 1, \ldots m$$

$$\sum_{i=1}^{n} x_i C_{ij} \leq U_j, \qquad j = 1, \ldots m$$

$$\sum_{i=1}^{n} x_i \leq 1$$

$$d_j^+ \geq 0, \qquad j = 1, \ldots m$$

$$d_j^- \geq 0, \qquad j = 1, \ldots m$$

$$x_i \geq 0, \qquad i = 1, \ldots n,$$

where

n is the available number of assets,

m is the number of different portfolio attributes,

x_i is the fraction of the portfolio held in asset i,

G_j is the target value or goal for portfolio attribute j,

$d_j{}^+$ and $d_j{}^-$ are positive and negative deviations from targets,

$P_j{}^+$ and $P_j{}^-$ are penalties for deviation from target G_j,

D_p is the weighted sum of deviations from the targets,

L_j is the minimum acceptable level of portfolio attribute j,

U_j is the maximum acceptable level of portfolio attribute j, and

C_{ij} is a measure of asset i's level of attribute j.

The above *goal program* is a special type of *linear program*, since its objective function to be minimized and each of its constraints are linear. The first three sets of constraints define deviations from attribute goals and upper and lower portfolio attribute bounds. The fourth constraint serves to limit the total portfolio investment to no more than 100% of the investor's wealth. The remaining constraints ensure that investment and deviation variables do not take on negative values.

The goal programming approach to portfolio selection is best suited to situations in which investment goals are predetermined or in which it is possible to elicit a clear statement of goals from the investor. Thus, this approach is potentially useful for personal investment advising, in which a relatively small number of assets (such as mutual funds of different types) are being considered (e.g., see Cohen and Lieberman 1983, and Puelz and Puelz 1989), and for implementing conformance, tactical, and scenario investing in an objective and systematic fashion.

In addition to the factors discussed in the last section, relevant goals might include desired levels of interest and dividend income, expected portfolio appreciation and riskiness, amount of income taxable in the current period, preservation of capital, the probability of experiencing a loss of capital, and desired sector, industry, and country participation levels. The goal programming model is a logical approach to resolving conflicts among such diverse goals. In addition, goal programming can be combined with other optimization approaches, including Mean-Variance optimization, which will be discussed next.

3.3   MEAN-VARIANCE OPTIMIZATION

3.3.1   The Markowitz Model

Probably the most universally accepted approach to portfolio selection today is the Mean-Variance Optimization approach introduced by Harry Markowitz (1952). In the basic Markowitz model, portfolio selection is represented by the following optimization problem:

$$\text{Minimize} \quad V_p = \sum_{i=1}^{n} \sum_{j=1}^{n} \sigma_{ij} x_i x_j \qquad (3.1)$$
$$X$$

or equivalently,

$$V_p = \sum_{i=1}^{n} \sigma_i^2 x_i^2 + \sum_{i=1}^{n} \sum_{\substack{j=1 \\ j \ne i}}^{n} \sigma_{ij} x_i x_j,$$

subject to

$$\sum_{i=1}^{n} R_i x_i = R_p \qquad (3.2)$$

$$\sum_{i=1}^{n} x_i = 1 \qquad (3.3)$$

$$x_i \ge 0, \quad i = 1, \ldots n, \qquad (3.4)$$

where

n is the number of available securities,

x_i is the fraction of the portfolio held in security i,

$R_i \equiv E(r_i)$ is the expected value of return on security i,

$R_p \equiv E(r_p)$ is a target level of expected return on the portfolio,

σ_i^2 is the variance of returns of security i

σ_{ij} is the covariance of returns of securities i and j, and

V_p is the variance of the portfolio's return.

In this problem, which is called a quadratic program or QP, the goal is to minimize the riskiness or variance V_p of the entire portfolio while achieving the minimally acceptable expected return R_p imposed by constraint (3.2). Constraint (3.3) ensures that available wealth is fully allocated, and the n non-negativity constraints (3.4) ensure that only a positive or zero investment is made in each security. If short selling was permissible for some subset of securities, the non-negativity constraint for those securities would be omitted. The objective function (3.1) is quadratic and the constraints are linear. Several highly efficient algorithms are available for solving this problem.[1] Portfolio risk is also commonly represented by the standard deviations σ_p, which as the square root of variance is a monotonically increasing function of V_p.

When R_p is varied parametrically, solutions to the QP model result in a set of efficient points representing portfolios with the property of minimal V_p and thus minimal σ_p for given expected return or, equivalently, maximum return for a given level of σ_p. These are called *efficient portfolios*. An alternative formulation of the risk-return optimization problem is

$$\text{Minimize}\atop X \quad V_p = \theta \sum_{i=1}^{n} \sum_{j=1}^{n} \sigma_{ij} x_i x_j - (1 - \theta) \sum_{i=1}^{n} R_i x_i$$

subject to

$$\sum_{i=1}^{n} x_i = 1$$

$$x_i \geq 0, \quad i = 1, \ldots n.$$

In this formulation θ is a weighting parameter. When this QP is solved for every value of θ between 0 and 1, the entire set of feasible efficient points is generated.

3.3.2   The Efficient Frontier

Collectively, the set of efficient points defines a line referred to as the *efficient frontier* (Figure 3.1). Enlarging the universe of assets from which the portfolio selection is made never results in a lower efficient

Figure 3.1
Efficient Risk-Return Frontier

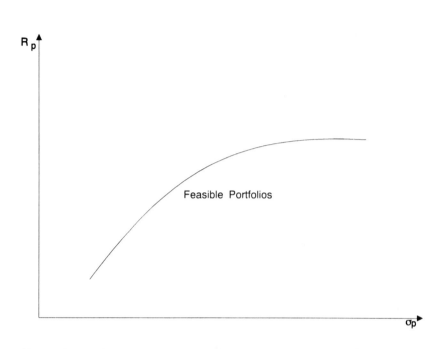

frontier, since new securities can always be included at a level of zero. By including in a portfolio assets whose returns are not highly positively correlated with those of other assets, investors may develop significantly improved risk-return combinations. This explains the current trend toward global investing and the inclusion of real estate and other nontraditional assets in the portfolios of major institutional investors.

Which portfolio is chosen from among those on the efficient frontier will depend on the investor's *utility function*, which represents preferences with respect to risk and return. As discussed in Chapter 2, different investors facing an identical efficient frontier are likely to choose efficient portfolios having at least somewhat differing levels of risk and return.

Viewing R_p as a function of σ_p, the efficient frontier $R(\sigma)$ will be *concave* over its range. This is because if any of the points $R(x'), \sigma(x')$ were to lie on a locally convex portion of the efficient frontier, they would be dominated with respect to risk and return by a portfolio comprising a linear combination of two portfolios, x^a and x^b, just on either side of that point. That is,

$$\left| R(\theta\, x^a + (1-\theta)x^b), -\sigma(\theta x^a + (1-\theta)x^b) \right| \geq \left| R(x'), -\sigma(x') \right|$$

for at least some value of θ such that $0 \leq \theta \leq 1$. If portfolio risk were measured by variance V_p rather than by standard deviation σ_p, the efficient frontier given by $R_p(V_p)$ would be *strictly concave* because $\sigma = \sqrt{V}$ is a strictly concave function, and a strictly concave function of a concave function is also strictly concave.

3.3.3   Model Enhancement

The basic Markowitz model can be embellished with additional constraints. For example, if it is determined that no more than fraction F_K of the portfolio should be invested in securities k of one or more industries K, additional constraints can be added of the form

$$\sum_{k\in K} x_k \leq F_K, \quad K = 1, \ldots$$

The basic Markowitz model can produce solutions with hundreds of securities included in the portfolio, some at levels approaching or even exceeding the total number of shares available and others at levels so small that their inclusion is uneconomic due to the high transaction costs of placing small orders. Therefore it may be desirable to limit the degree of diversification in some way. To restrict the portfolio to no more than N different securities, the Markowitz model could, for example, be augmented with the following $2n + 1$ constraints:

$$x_i - y_i \leq 0, \quad i = 1, \ldots n$$

$$\sum_{i=1}^{n} y_i \leq N$$

$$y_i = 0,1 \quad i = 1, \ldots n.$$

Here the y_i variables are restricted to the values of zero or one, and the problem becomes a *mixed zero-one integer program*, whose solution requires specialized optimization algorithms. (For other limited diversification models, see Faaland 1974.)

It is fairly easy to incorporate linear transaction costs into the Markowitz model; in this case, the transaction cost associated with security i is assumed to diminish its expected return R_i by δ_i percent. For security i already held in amount W_i, the amount to be purchased or sold can be represented by the non-negative variables x_i^+ and x_i^-. For each security a constraint is added of the form

$$x_i - W_i - x_i^+ + x_i^- = 0,$$

and the expression for net expected return

$$R_i x_i - \delta_i (x_i^+ + x_i^-)$$

is substituted in place of each of the $R_i x_i$'s in constraint (3.2) of the basic model.

3.4   BETA AND INDEX MODELS

If the Markowitz model is used to select from a universe of thousands of securities, there will be difficulties associated with data acquisition. Nevertheless, investors have successfully used simple but effective computerized mean-variance optimization systems that limit investment allocation decisions to a few broad classes of asset types, such as domestic and foreign stocks, bonds, and bills, or to economic sectors, such as capital goods, consumer, and business-cycle sensitive (e.g., see Franks 1990).

Sharpe (1963) developed a practical answer to the problem of computing numerous stock return covariances. His method requires knowing both the covariance of each security i with an index I representing the market, and the *beta coefficient* for each security. Beta measures the responsiveness of the security's return to the return r_I of the index, and can be viewed as the slope of the linear equation

$$r_i = \alpha_i + \beta_i r_I,$$

which is called the security's *characteristic line*.

The value of beta in this equation can in principle be estimated by regressing historical security returns against returns on the index, using the estimating equation

$$r_{it} = \alpha_i + \beta_i \, r_{It} + \varepsilon_{it} \, ,$$

where ε_{it} is the residual for each observation t, representing the variation in security return not explained by variations in the market. Beta is said to measure the *systematic* or *market risk* of an asset. This source of risk cannot be reduced or eliminated through diversification without a diminishment of expected return, so it is also called *nondiversifiable risk*.

The portion of a security's risk that is represented statistically by the residuals, specifically the magnitude of the sum of their squares in relation to the security return variance, is called *unsystematic, company-specific,* or *diversifiable* risk. This source of risk *can* be reduced by diversification, since the residuals of a collection of securities, when summed together, will tend to cancel one another out.

Another way of looking at this is to examine the variance of the return of a collection of securities that is not explained by variations in the return of the index. This unexplained variance, represented by σ_u^2, will decrease as the number of securities increases. The covariances of the residuals of securities i and j can be represented by $\sigma_{\varepsilon_i \varepsilon_j}$. It is reasonable to expect the values of $\sigma_{\varepsilon_i \varepsilon_j}$ for $i \neq j$ to be randomly distributed, and about half to be of positive and half of negative sign. If each of n securities is held in equal fractional amounts $1/n$, the unexplained collective return variance is

$$\sigma_u^2 = \sum_{i=1}^{n} \sum_{j=1}^{n} (1/n)^2 \, \sigma_{\varepsilon_i \varepsilon_j}$$

or, equivalently,

$$\sigma_u^2 = (1/n)^2 \sum_{i=1}^{n} \sigma_{\varepsilon_i}^2 + (1/n)^2 \sum_{i=1}^{n} \sum_{\substack{j=1 \\ j \neq i}}^{n} \sigma_{\varepsilon_i \varepsilon_j} \, ,$$

where $\sigma_{\varepsilon_i}^2$ is the residual variance for security i.

To see how unsystematic risk can be diversified away, we need only impose the relatively weak assumption that the *average* of the $\sigma_{\varepsilon_i \varepsilon_j}$'s, $i \neq j$, is zero. Under this assumption, $\sigma_u^2 \to 0$ as $n \to \infty$. This occurs because the second term of the above expression approaches zero through the cancellation of positive and negative covariances, and the first term approaches zero because the factor $(1/n)^2$ decreases at a rate faster than the linear rate at which new elements are added to the summation. Empirical studies of small portfolios of both human-selected and randomly selected stocks have shown that nearly all of the unsystematic risk has been eliminated when $n \geq 30$.

A logical source of data for estimating beta via regression would be observed pairs of daily, weekly, or monthly security and index prices from the recent past. Since it is future beta that matters for portfolio decisions, more sophisticated methodologies have been proposed for developing accurate forecasts of betas (e.g., see Rosenberg and Guy 1976 and Elton, Gruber, and Urich 1978). Beta estimates computed using differing methodologies and with a variety of adjustments are available from commercial services for stocks listed on major exchanges; note that betas can be computed for portfolios as well as for securities.

For securities highly correlated with some index having return variance σ_I^2, the product $\beta_i \beta_j \sigma_I^2$ provides a good estimate of covariance σ_{ij}. The computational burden of generating objective function parameters for the Markowitz model can be greatly reduced by using this relationship, as only n betas plus the index variance need to be computed, instead of n security variances and $n(n-1)/2$ covariances of every security against every other. (Division is by 2 because $\sigma_{ij} \equiv \sigma_{ji}$.)

If the only common source of variation in individual security returns is the market return, then the covariance of the residuals of every security with those of every other security will be zero ($\sigma_{\varepsilon_i \varepsilon_j} = 0$, $i \neq j$), and the quadratic optimization problem can be greatly simplified at the expense of adding just one new variable and constraint. Under this assumption, the Markowitz objective function can be rewritten as

$$V_p = \sigma_I^2 \left(\sum_{i=1}^{n} \beta_i x_i \right)^2 + \sum_{i=1}^{n} \sigma_{\varepsilon_i}^2 x_i^2 \, ;$$

or, equivalently, by substituting z for the weighted average β, as

$$V_p = \sigma_I^2 z^2 + \sum_{i=1}^{n} \sigma_{\varepsilon_i}^2 x_i^2,$$

where the linear constraint

$$\sum_{i=1}^{n} \beta_i x_i - z = 0$$

is added to the basic model. Rather than comprising a dense $n \times n$ matrix, the objective function now consists of only n diagonal matrix elements plus the term associated with index return variance.

The index-model approach can readily be extended to multiple indexes. Analogous to the characteristic line would be a plane or hyperplane that best fits security returns to the returns of two or more indexes. A multiple regression of security returns against several indexes (also called factors), results in a beta for each security with respect to each index ($\beta(1)_i$, $\beta(2)_i$, $\beta(3)_i$, etc.) plus residuals representing, as before, the unsystematic risk that is not explainable by movements in these indexes. In addition to the market-return index, indexes of inflation rate, money supply, or other economic variables may be employed. It is important that the indexes themselves not be highly correlated, or little improvement will result over the single-market index model. If indexes are carefully chosen, the resulting portfolios should not be greatly suboptimal in risk and expected return to those that would be chosen using Markowitz's original model.

3.5   SECURITY RISK AND PORTFOLIO RISK

Total portfolio risk is given by σ_p, which includes both systematic and unsystematic risk components. The more diversified the portfolio the smaller its unsystematic risk, which approaches zero for highly diversified portfolios. The risk of a security i whose returns are totally uncorrelated with other assets in a portfolio could be adequately represented by σ_i. Such securities are rare. Most securities have returns that are correlated with others, if for no other reason than that they are jointly dependent on the market; thus, the riskiness of a particular security must be viewed in relation to that of all the other securities in the portfolio.

Since diversifying a portfolio by combining securities is possible, at least in principle, for all investors, the *relevant risk* of a security's being added to a portfolio is related to the security's impact on the systematic risk of the portfolio. This is represented collectively by security i's covariances with the other securities in the portfolio, or in a short-hand way by the effect of its inclusion on the portfolio's beta.

Portfolios have many of the same characteristics as individual securities, that is, expected returns, standard deviations, and betas. The beta of portfolio P plus security A is given by the weighted average of their betas (i.e., $\beta_{P+A} = x_P \beta_P + x_A \beta_A$, where $x_P + x_A = 1$); depending on the security's beta relative to that of the portfolio, its addition may increase or decrease the portfolio's systematic risk.

Therefore, both securities and portfolios should be priced such that those with progressively greater systematic risk or beta offer greater expected return; at the same time, expected returns should be independent of unsystematic risk, since this risk can be virtually eliminated by further diversification. There is a great deal of empirical evidence supporting this proposition. The functional relationship between expected return and beta is represented by a line called the *security market line*, which will be precisely defined in the next section.

3.6   THE ROLE OF RISKLESS ASSETS

Most conventional treatments of portfolio theory introduce a riskless asset into the risk-return space (see Figure 3.2). This asset is represented by a point on the vertical axis. In the Finance literature, one-month Treasury bills are often assumed to be riskless assets, because they are guaranteed by the federal government, they are of such short maturity as to pose negligible maturity risk, and they have a highly liquid secondary market. Since a portfolio can consist of a combination of riskless and risky assets, every point on the straight line beginning at R_f and tangent to the Markowitz efficient frontier represents some feasible portfolio. The point of tangency M is that of a portfolio called the *market portfolio*. Its expected return is R_m and its risk is σ_m. The market portfolio's beta is 1, and the beta of a portfolio or index that approximates the market portfolio ought to be close to 1.[2] Points to the right of the market

---

Figure 3.2
Efficient Frontier and Capital-Market Line

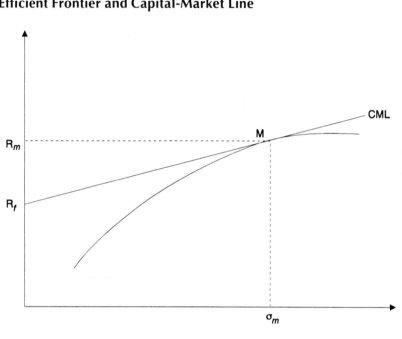

portfolio are efficient risk-return combinations achievable only if one can borrow at the risk-free rate.[3]

Thus the riskless asset serves to linearize the risk-return combinations available to the investor. The resultant line is called the *capital market line*, or *CML*. The equation for the CML is

$$R(\sigma) = R_f + (R_m - R_f)\, \sigma/\sigma_m .$$

Since market risk can be eliminated through diversification, the only relevant risk of *individual securities* is beta, and it follows that in market equilibrium the expected return of an individual security i ought to be a function of only its beta risk, the risk-free rate R_f, and the market risk premium, $R_m - R_f$. The relationship is given by the security market line or *SML*,

$$R_i = R_f + \beta_i (R_m - R_f).$$

These relationships between expected return and risk are the basis for the *capital-asset pricing model* (CAPM), developed independently by Sharpe (1964), Mossin (1965), and Lintner (1966). The CAPM can be used in a normative fashion to determine the required risk-return characteristics of assets in a variety of settings, both internal and external to a firm.[4]

The CAPM can be extended to consider other measures of portfolio performance. In addition to expected return and risk, investors are likely to have preferences with respect to skewness or other higher return distribution moments (Rubinstein 1973, Kraus and Litzenberger 1973) and the probability of return below zero or below that achievable without risk. These issues become significant when portfolios are frequently rebalanced using a dynamic strategy. One must then select not only an efficient portfolio, but also an *efficient dynamic allocation strategy* from those which lie on a *capital-market surface* (Trippi and Harriff 1991).

3.7   MEAN ABSOLUTE DEVIATION OPTIMIZATION

The assumption of variance or standard deviation as the primary portfolio risk measure may be rejected completely, as in models that define portfolio risk as the *mean absolute deviation* (*MAD*) of returns from their expected values, or

$$E(|r_p - R_p|).$$

Konno and Yamazaki (1991) have shown that minimizing a portfolio's mean absolute deviation is equivalent to minimizing its standard deviation when portfolio returns are generated by a multivariate normal process.

In addition to having a superior correlation with subjective assessments of risk, the MAD model has several advantages over the Markowitz or index model QP's. It can be formulated as a linear program that permits portfolio optimization over a much larger asset universe for a given level of computational effort; it generally produces a smaller number of securities at positive levels in optimal portfolios; and it does not require the prior computation of large covariance matrices.

A capital-asset pricing model analogous to the conventional CAPM can be constructed using the mean absolute deviation risk measure, in which equilibrium prices of individual securities are given by

$$R_i = R_f + \mu_i (R_m - R_f),$$

and the derived parameter μ has an interpretation similar to that of beta. With securities selected from those included in the Nikkei 225 index, Konno and Yamazaki found that the dense-matrix Markowitz model's efficient frontier and security mixes were closer to those of the MAD model than to those of a single-index Sharpe-type model.

3.8   MARKOWITZ AND CAPITAL-ASSET PRICING MODEL LIMITATIONS

There is evidence that the CAPM, in both its standard form and with distribution parameter extensions, is an incomplete model of asset pricing. That is, not all of the expected return of efficient portfolios can be explained by their standard deviation, variance, or higher distribution moments, and not all of the expected returns of individual securities are explainable by their betas.

The *arbitrage pricing theory* (APT) model (Ross 1976) attempts to address some of these shortcomings by postulating that expected returns on assets are a function of several *factors*; and that an arbitrage process will drive the prices of assets up or down so that if assets have a similar response to movements in these factors, they will offer similar returns. In other words, there may be several sources of systematic risk common to most securities. Although the price movement of the market as a whole is a significant (and probably dominant) factor in the expected returns of individual securities, the APT model does not say specifically which other factors ought to be considered; however, it does relax some of the CAPM's assumptions about investor preferences, while imposing the requirement that the return-generating function be linearly separable with respect to its components. Considerable empirical research has been directed to verifying the APT model; a more comprehensive treatment of both the CAPM and the APT models may be found in standard texts such as Elton and Gruber (1987), Haugen (1986), Sharpe (1985), and Reilly (1985).

From a practical standpoint, a more serious problem with using the Markowitz model or the CAPM for portfolio selection is that neither provides a mechanism for incorporating superior knowledge of industries, companies, products, corporate management, or market anomalies into portfolio-mix decisions. These decisions can have a profound effect on ex post portfolio returns. Many assets possess negligible risk yet have returns slightly superior than those of Treasury bills. These assets are near-substitutes at the low-risk end of the spectrum.

At greater levels of risk, near-substitutes are assets that have covariances similar to those of other assets in the market portfolio. Given that there are thousands of securities to choose from, one would expect to find many near-substitutes among risky assets, or a certain amount of redundancy in efficient portfolios. Small departures from the theoretically optimal mix of many securities, or large departures in the case of a smaller number of near-substitutes, will have little impact on the ex ante level of portfolio risk for a given expected return. This is depicted by line EA in Figure 3.3, which reverses the amounts invested in some near-substitute pairs in each of the portfolios on the efficient frontier EF. Knowledge that results in superior estimates of future returns of individual securities (or future returns of the market as a whole) could easily outweigh the small loss of expected return from following an investment policy that is technically suboptimal in the CAPM framework, with the end result being an ex post frontier such as line EP. Later chapters of this book will discuss how such knowledge is represented and incorporated into the portfolio selection process.

ENDNOTES

1. The objective function is convex if the matrix $\|\sigma_{ij}\|$ is positive semidefinite. One of the earliest algorithms to solve this problem was the modified simplex method of Wolfe (1959), which is still in use. Those familiar with mathematical optimization will note that the Kuhn-Tucker optimality conditions for the Markowitz QP comprise a set of linear equalities, plus a set of pairs of dual and slack variables whose products must equal zero (complementary slackness). These conditions can be achieved by solving a linear program (LP) that drives "artificial" variables to zero, while maintaining complementary slackness. The essence of Wolfe's method is to solve the Kuhn-Tucker equations by using the ordi-

Figure 3.3
Ex Ante and Ex Post Frontiers

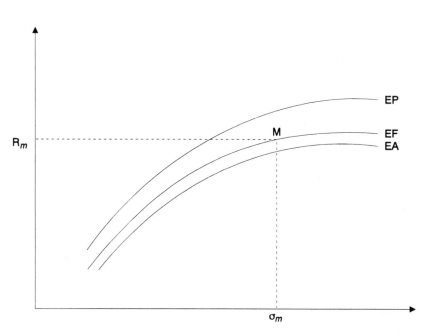

nary LP simplex algorithm augmented with additional checks to determine whether each prescribed pivot operation will maintain the required complementary slackness condition. Whenever a normal pivot would result in a violation of complementary slackness, the next-best variable is brought into the basis instead. Programs for solving QP problems are widely available, including inexpensive student versions of the most popular software packages capable of solving problems with several dozen variables and constraints.

2. If all investors are rational in the Markowitz sense, then they should invest in risky assets only in the mix given by the market portfolio. Market clearing of risky assets would require that the market portfolio include each risky asset in exact proportion to its value, or price times number of shares outstanding. Under these

assumptions, the market portfolio would represent a value-weighted security index.

3. If borrowing is possible only at an interest rate greater than R_f, the portion of the CML to the right of point M will be a straight line through that borrowing rate on the vertical axis and tangent to the Markowitz efficient frontier. This results in a downward bend in the CML beyond point M. If the risk-free asset is not included in the market portfolio, the return on a zero-beta portfolio is sometimes used in place of R_f in the capital-asset pricing model.

4. For individual securities one would expect to find empirically, that

$$r_{it} = R_f + \beta_i (R_m - R_f) + \varepsilon_{it},$$

where $E(\varepsilon_i) = 0$. If $E(\varepsilon_i) > 0$, the security exhibits *excess returns to beta*, a disequilibrium condition that is considered an anomaly within the CAPM framework.

REFERENCES

Cohen, P., and Lieberman, M., 1983. "A Report on Folio: an Expert Assistant for Portfolio Managers." *Proceedings of the International Joint Conference on Artificial Intelligence* 212–14.

Elton, E. J., and Gruber, M. J., 1987. *Modern Portfolio Theory and Investment Analysis*. New York: Wiley.

Elton, E., Gruber, M., and Urich, T., 1978. "Are Betas Best?" *The Journal of Finance* 13, 5 (December): 1375–84.

Faaland, B., 1974. "An Integer Programming Algorithm for Portfolio Selection." *Management Science* 20, 10 (June): 1376–88.

Franks, E. "A Decision Support System for Revision of Portfolios to Achieve Pre-Specified Real Returns with Reliability and Efficiency," in Trippi, R., and Turban, E., eds., 1990, *Investment Management: Decision Support and Expert Systems*. New York: Van Nostrand Reinhold.

Haugen, R. A., 1986. *Modern Investment Theory*. Englewood Cliffs, N.J.: Prentice Hall.

Ignizio, J. P., 1976. *Goal Programming and Extensions*. Lexington, MA: Lexington Books.

Konno, H., and Yamazaki, H., 1991. "Mean-Absolute Deviation Portfolio Optimization Model and Its Applications to the Tokyo Stock Market." *Management Science* 37, 5 (May): 519–31.

Kraus, A., and Litzenberger, R., 1976. "Skewness Preference and the Valuation of Risky Assets." *The Journal of Finance* 31 (September): 1085–1100.

Lintner, J., 1965. "Security Prices, Risk, and Maximal Gains from Diversification." *The Journal of Finance* (December): 587–615.

Markowitz, H., 1952. "Portfolio Selection." *The Journal of Finance* 7 (March): 77–91.

Mossin, J., 1966. "Equilibrium in a Capital Market." *Econometrica* 34 (October): 768–83.

Puelz, A., and Puelz, R., 1989. "Personal Financial Planning: an Interactive Goal Programming Model Using U-Shaped Penalty Functions." *Proceedings, 1989 Annual Meeting,* Decision Sciences Institute, New Orleans, 327–29.

Reilly, F. K., 1985. *Investment Analysis and Portfolio Management.* New York: Dryden Press.

Rosenberg, B., and Guy, J., 1976. "Prediction of Beta from Investment Fundamentals – Part I." *Financial Analysts Journal* 32, 4 (May–June): 60–72.

Rosenberg, B., and Guy, J., 1976. "Prediction of Beta from Investment Fundamentals – Part 2." *Financial Analysts Journal* 32, 4 (July–August): 62–70.

Ross, S. A., 1976. "The Arbitrage Theory of Capital Asset Pricing." *Journal of Economic Theory* (December).

Rubinstein, M., 1973. "The Fundamental Theorem of Parameter-Preference Security Valuation." *Journal of Financial and Quantitative Analysis* 8 (January): 61–9.

Sharpe, W. F., 1963. "A Simplified Model for Portfolio Analysis." *Management Science* 9, 2 (January): 277–93.

Sharpe, W. F., 1964. "Capital Asset Prices: A Theory of Market Equilibrium Under Conditions of Risk." *The Journal of Finance* 19 (September): 425–42.

Sharpe, W. F., 1985. *Investments.* Englewood Cliffs, N.J.: Prentice Hall.

Trippi, R., and Harriff, R., 1991. "Dynamic Asset Allocation Rules: Survey and Synthesis." *The Journal of Portfolio Management* 17, 4 (Summer).

Wolfe, P., 1959. "The Simplex Method for Quadratic Programming." *Econometrica* 27: 382–98.

CHAPTER 4

Knowledge-Based Systems in Investment Management: An Overview

4.1   PROGRAMMED VS. AUTO-LEARNING SYSTEMS[1]

This chapter discusses, in a very general way, the nature of knowledge-based systems and how they can be applied to investment decision making, and gives examples of applications. Knowledge-based systems are generally divided into *programmed* and *auto-learning systems.* Programmed systems require the explicit input of decision rules in order to acquire knowledge; most conventionally implemented expert systems fall into this category. Auto-learning systems program themselves through exposure to attribute-outcome examples, and may be "trained" with either test data or a subset of actual (i.e., historical) data. A common way to validate the performance of an auto-learning system prior to implementing it is to measure the proportion of correct decisions that are made on the remaining subset of actual data.

The adjustment of decision rules and/or system parameters in response to the ex post performance of an auto-learning system is illustrated in Figure 4.1. Among the ways in which conventionally implemented expert systems can operate in an auto-learning mode, one is through *rule induction* or *learning-from-example* (LFE). In recent years, the technology referred to as *neural networks* or *artificial neural systems* has also been used to develop expert systems capable of learning. Mechanisms of learning in auto-learning systems are generally referred to as *machine learning* processes. These will be discussed in more detail in Chapter 9.

4.2   AN INTRODUCTION TO KNOWLEDGE REPRESENTATION

Knowledge representation, goals, and methodology are the major components of problem representation. Talluru and Ackgiray (1990) describe the solution process as involving three steps: (1) *abstraction,* (2) *structuring,* and (3) *model selection.* In this process, the *size* of the problem space (Newell and Simon 1972), its *character,* and the *solution methodology* all place economic limits on the scope of problem that can be solved. In a knowledge-based system, the character of the solution space is defined primarily by the way that knowledge is represented.

Knowledge representation is a formalism for the systematic computer storage of facts and rules about a subject or specialty. In programmed systems, knowledge usually comes from human experts. A person who encodes the knowledge into the knowledge base is called, in

Figure 4.1
Auto-Learning Expert System

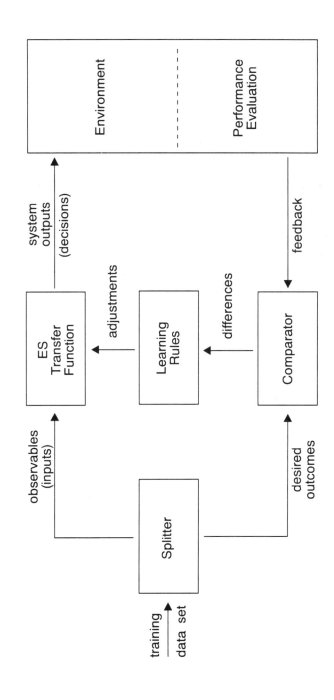

Source: Trippi (1990)

ES jargon, a knowledge engineer. The process of knowledge acquisition often requires that the knowledge engineer interview, observe, and interact with domain experts. This process known as knowledge engineering, can be difficult and time-consuming. In auto-learning systems, in contrast, knowledge acquisition may take place through the system's analyzing examples by itself, without the presence of a domain expert.

Knowledge may be represented in conventional ESs in a number of ways. The most common representations are known as *production rules, semantic networks,* and *frames.* Production (condition-action) rule representation is the most frequently encountered approach in commercial ESs, and the one that will be focused on in this book. Rules may be implemented through either logic-based computer languages such as PROLOG, or the use of an ES *inference engine* or *shell,* an application software package that frees the user from doing detailed computer programming tasks. By using an ES shell, one may explicitly enter knowledge and inference rules into the knowledge base in a form close to that of natural language. The following are examples of rules that might be included in a hypothetical portfolio management knowledge base:

IF   the price of gold is less than the 4-year average

AND   the inflation rate exceeds the T-bill rate

THEN   include 15% gold in the portfolio;

(knowledge rule)

or

IF   index has moved more than 12 points from last rebalance

THEN   rebalance cash to stocks using formula #1;

(knowledge rule)

or

IF   dollar-yen exchange rate is not in the system

THEN   request it from the user.

(inference rule)

In a rule-based ES, the subset and sequence of knowledge rules that "fire," or have their antecedents fulfilled, will depend upon the user's answers to a series of critical questions asked by the ES. Rule-based ESs may have hundreds or even thousands of questions and rules available in the knowledge base. The final action recommendation of such a "consultant" ES is called its *goal*. We will discuss more complex types of rules in later chapters.

In an auto-learning rule-based system, rules are developed through the use of algorithms that best match problem attributes and goals, or that select the most effective rule subset from a larger set of potential rules. Through data-driven induction, a rule structure is developed to satisfy a given set of instances. Conflicts may be resolved by nesting mediating rules within earlier derived rules, or by using heuristic procedures that reform the tentative rule set. In model-driven induction, rejection of rules in an a priori set would be guided by the tolerance for misclassification of test examples. In using this type of induction, a human expert must often be called upon to review the remaining rules for consistency and bias. In certain domains, the rule induction procedure can be formalized. For example, Holsapple, Whinston, and Tam (1988) have developed a methodology for updating rule sets for security trading that generates new rules by simply running the procedures on new examples as they arrive. In a conventional ES the successive invocation of rules partitions the output, or goal-set, into complex, though usually linearly separable, regions (see Figure 4.2).

In contrast, neural network-based expert systems do not employ explicit rules. The mechanism by which relevant attributes result in outputs, such as action recommendations, is more subtle. The final input-output mapping will depend upon the topology of the network, node transfer functions, and network interconnect weights that result from training. Knowledge is diffused throughout the network, and is represented by the interconnect weights in only a collective sense. There may be thousands or even millions of such weights. Therefore, unlike conventionally implemented expert systems, neural networks do not easily provide explanatory insights. Nevertheless, there do exist specialized software products that derive explanation from networks with varying degrees of success. Learning and other aspects of neural network ESs will be discussed in more detail later in this chapter and in Chapter 9.

4.3   EXPERT SYSTEMS AND FINANCIAL SERVICES

Considerable success has been reported in recent years in applying conventional ESs to routine financial decision-making operations such as

Figure 4.2
Partitioning of ES Output Set (with outputs *A, B, C, D*)

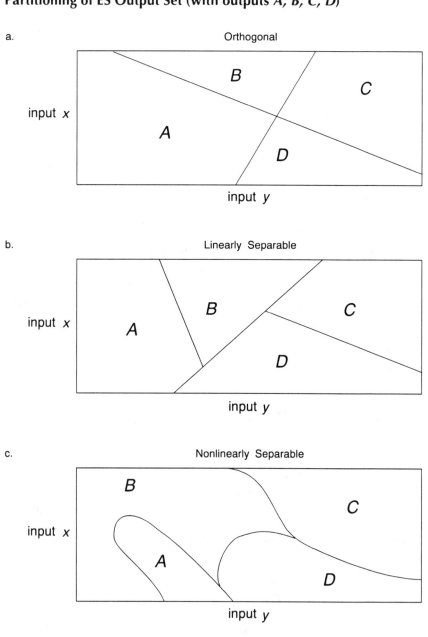

approval of credit lines, mortgage underwriting, financial planning, and the underwriting of complex insurance policies (e.g., see Bestor 1987, Shannon 1985, Sviokla 1988, and the survey by Friedland 1988). These activities involve risk assessment, which is a generalization problem. Active portfolio management, on the other hand, includes elements of recognition (seizing opportunities) as well as generalization. In order to be successful, ES for such an application must have a considerably greater degree of sophistication than a pure generalization system.

The portfolio management process involves a number of stages amenable to ES. These include the following (adapted from Talluru and Akgiray 1988):

- Identification of goals and constraints
- Generation of set of feasible investments
- Formulation of alternative strategies
- Selection of an appropriate strategy
- Implementation of the selected strategy
- Explanation of results and consultation

Not all portfolio management ESs need perform all of these functions. Goals, constraints, and even the strategy may be predetermined exogenously to the ES (e.g., by using the philosophy or charter of the investing entity or sponsor). In many applications, the ES's primary functions are limited to implementation and explanation.

Areas of portfolio management for which ES technology holds the greatest promise include the following:

- Static asset diversification (or asset allocation) decisions
- Market timing decisions
- Implementation of dynamic diversification and hedging strategies (e.g., portfolio insurance)
- The systematic application of inclusion/exclusion criteria to specific asset classes.

Static diversification involves selecting a portfolio that is likely to meet specific investment goals. When the investments are of a long-term nature, the portfolio may need to be revised only infrequently. Therefore, the primary use of an ES for this purpose might be to elicit investment goals and make long-term investment commitments.

Buy-sell timing decisions for individual assets (or asset classes) are especially amenable to the ES approach, since the goal (but not necessarily the set of rules) lacks complexity. Typically, investment experts use various cues or factors to make timing decisions, and these cues or factors can often be elicited through interviews or induced from examples.

Dynamic strategies involve making incremental rather than wholesale changes to the portfolio. These may be directed through interaction with an ES; for example, one could rebalance a portfolio between cash and stock index futures in a constant-proportion insurance strategy. The purchase and sale of options as a hedging mechanism could also be categorized as a dynamic strategy because of the relatively short-term nature of such hedges. Yet another example of a dynamic strategy is to continually revise optimally diversified portfolios in response to an incoming stream of relevant data.

For prescreening, ESs can also be constructed that will systematically and consistently apply inclusion criteria (in addition to risk and return) to specific asset classes; for example, a manager of commercial real estate investments could select projects from a short list generated with the assistance of an ES that employs expert-derived criteria related to location, type, size, age, projected financial performance and so on. The next system to be discussed implements such screening operations quite effectively.

4.4   AN EARLY ES FOR PORTFOLIO SELECTION

Clarkson (1963) was one of the earliest researchers to attempt to apply artificial intelligence to investment decision making, with a system that allowed a computer to imitate a manager's selection of common stocks for bank trust-fund portfolios. The human who was managing these funds used criteria such as the stocks' quality (e.g., whether or not they were held by another leading trust institution) and historical performance record to make selections. With the system developed by Clarkson, more than two-thirds of the stocks chosen by the computer for four test accounts, ranging from income to high growth, were identical to those selected by the human. The remainder were in the same industry group and of similar risk. As the stocks were chosen for long-term investment, this was essentially a static diversification problem.

The system operated in several stages. First, an "A" list of stocks was created, based on the current value of each stock, as well as its average value over ten years and the rate of change of that value. Expectations relating to the economy, industry, and ten company attributes, were also factored in. Next a relative value list, based on a three-year forecast of earnings per share, was created; from this list a set of "B" list stocks was drawn up for potential inclusion in each common and individual account. Which stocks were selected for this "B" list depended upon the account's specific goals.

From a historical perspective, the success of Clarkson's system is remarkable, considering that ES programming languages and shells were not available at the time. By the mid-1980s, the widespread availability of such tools had caused both investors and academicians to take renewed interest in ES applications for investment management as well as for other fields.

4.5   CONTEMPORARY SYSTEMS

As security analysis is a time-consuming and error-prone process, it can be improved considerably by automation. In 1988, Kandt and Yuenger developed an ES workstation that could help an operator perform technical and fundamental analyses for stock selection. Kandt and Yuenger's system analyzes the signals generated by various indicators, oscillators, and indexes, determines the appropriateness of these signals in light of current economic conditions, and then makes acquisition and diversification decisions. Their system also incorporates interday heuristic rules related to statistical evidence, such as

IF   the first 5 trading days are up by 1%

THEN   the year will be up too, by about 20%

WITH   93% certainty;

intraday rules such as

IF   the opening has been strong

THEN   a sell-off may occur between 10:30 and 11:00

and rules related to recurring patterns in stock movements. Most of the data needed by the system is acquired electronically, which drastically reduces the tedium and errors associated with human input. Rules are validated by replaying past history against the knowledge base, with great latitude given for experimenting to see how new algorithms and heuristics perform on actual data.

One ES developed exclusively as an aid in recognizing investment opportunities is the Washington Square Advisors WATCHDOG Investment Monitoring System (Gerkey and Landerholm 1988). WATCHDOG screens commercially available financial data on over 7,000 companies through about fifteen financial ratios, and analyzes trends and changes in risk measures. Its knowledge base incorporates the experience and skills of two expert financial analysts who concentrate on corporate bond investments. A junior analyst using WATCHDOG was reportedly able to accomplish in an hour what it had previously taken experts weeks to do. An interesting financial-analysis application in a related domain is the LBOCON ES, which assesses the soundness of potential takeover candidates (Mostert, Chandra, and Rao 1989). Using rules based on publicly available financial ratios, this system identifies prospective candidates for leveraged buyouts.

Through electronic means, a large amount of economic and financial information can now be accessed rapidly and accurately. Rau (1988) describes a knowledge-based system for text retrieval, developed at GE's Corporate Research and Development Center, that signals potential takeover targets and other nonrecurring investment opportunities. The system, called SCISOR (System for Conceptual Information Summarization, Organization and Retrieval), was developed using the AI language LISP. Its function is to develop natural language synopses of the history of news releases in a particular domain from diverse sources, through the use of an array of novel mapping, pattern selection, and restriction operations. SCISOR produces summaries of activities such as stock-price movement, purchase offers, and status of transactions.

Having real-time data available is necessary in order to do most forms of program trading, including index arbitrage. Liang and Chen (1987) describe a prototype system used for this purpose, called PRO-TRADER. In this system, rules are developed for monitoring both trading and position unwinding signals from the market. The spot-future premium level is continuously compared with statistical limits computed from an analysis of recent premium means and standard deviations. The rules generate a sophisticated variance-based dynamic strategy that is highly responsive to changes in the volatility of the market.

In contrast to the relatively focused domains of opportunity-seizing systems, the knowledge bases of ES that assist in diversification usually do not require real-time, or even daily, maintenance. The purpose of these systems is to develop portfolios that not only meet certain industry or other diversification constraints, but are also risk-return efficient and capable of achieving other investment goals.

One such ES, called FOLIO is an expert assistant for professional money managers (Cohen and Lieberman 1983). FOLIO is used to allocate account assets across funds, rather than select individual securities. It employs nine asset classes, including high-growth stocks; dividend-oriented, low-growth stocks; tax-free bonds; and government and highly rated bonds. The average degree of risk and return in each fund is a known quantity.

The ES portion of FOLIO selects client goals and measures the importance of these to each account. There are fourteen types of goals, ranging from hedges to goals associated with balancing risk and income from different sources. FOLIO has three major components: a set of interview functions, a formal chaining production rule system for inferring clients' goals, and a goal-programming algorithm that minimizes the deviation of the portfolio from the goals that FOLIO is to satisfy. In this application, the ES only selects goals and their weights; the goal-programming algorithm allocates assets to various funds.

Another example of a successful contemporary commercial portfolio management ES is the LA-COURTIER security advisory system, developed by Cognitive Systems. In contrast to FOLIO, which was developed to assist the professional manager, LA-COURTIER is designed to assist wealthy individual investors who are customers of its sponsor, a Belgian bank. This ES performs many of the same functions that a portfolio advisory consultant would, thus saving the bank the expense of having to assign a trained investment counselor to each branch.

After interviewing customers to collect information about their financial situation, LA-COURTIER makes specific recommendations as to which stock and other investment purchases would be appropriate for each customer.

Users can interrupt the system to ask questions or express likes or dislikes; if a specific security recommendation is rejected by a customer, the system will revise the suggested portfolio, with that security or its industry group excluded. In addition, users can query the database for specific information, such as price or earnings, about individual securities.

Similar in function to the LA-COURTIER system is an ES called INVEST, which was developed for a large German bank (Heuer, Koch, and Cryer 1988). INVEST is a frame-based system that dialogues with bank officials when they make investment recommendations to their clients. Frames, which avoid the predicate redundancies sometimes seen in production rules, are an efficient means of representing knowledge. Frame-based systems employ the principle of inheritance, which makes it possible to define general facts only once. During a consultation with INVEST, information is first built up about the customer; this customer profile then determines any subsequent questions to be asked. The developers assert that all investment possibilities on the West German securities market can be represented by about 50 basic hypotheses, which the system seeks to validate or invalidate. The inference engine on which INVEST was developed employs a matching mechanism across frames that returns a number between −1000 (exact opposite) and +1000 (identical). The matching process is ideal for comparing a particular customer's profile with a prototype for which the appropriate advice has already been developed. Problems of effectively interfacing such consultant systems with the user are discussed in detail by King (1988). With the rapid growth of public and private corporate-sponsored personal financial planning in the 1990s, a huge market has developed for systems, such as Applied Expert Systems' popular Plan Power product, that "advise the advisor."

The potential of rule induction for improving investment timing decisions was shown in a study done by Braun and Chandler in 1987. In this study, which used an ES software package designed for this purpose, past examples of a market analyst's behavior were used to formulate decision rules. These rules were developed to predict the expert's in-and-out-of-market calls as well as actual market movement. This approach freed the knowledge engineer from having to elicit the decision model explicitly from the decision maker through a lengthy interview process.

The performance of the expert, who relied more on technical than on fundamental analysis to make predictions, was very good over the period examined, with average annual returns in excess of 40%. Potential cues included economic, financial, and subjective indexes and their direction of change. The rules induced from 60 examples accurately predicted the analyst's timing calls about 50% of the time, and accurately predicted market movements an average of 64.4% of the time. The latter predictive performance was approximately as good as that of the expert.

Other ESs that have been developed in recent years for portfolio selection include NYU's PMIDSS (Portfolio Management Intelligent Decision Support System) and the Athena Group's Portfolio Management advisor (see Lee and Stohr 1985, and Athena 1987). The PMIDSS approaches the problems of timing and selection simultaneously, but is still somewhat experimental, while the Portfolio Management Advisor is a commercial product that supports several portfolio management methodologies. Another early experimental system, ISPMS (Intelligent Stock Portfolio Management System), the precursor to the K-FOLIO ES described later in this book, integrates the Markowitz quadratic programming optimization model with representation and inference of an expert's personal preferences and knowledge (Lee, Trippi, Chu, and Kim 1990).

4.6   NEURAL NETWORKS

Neural networks differ radically from the algorithmic model used by conventional ES. Neural computation is massively parallel, typically employing from several hundred to millions of individual simple processors, arranged in a communicative network. Thus, the architecture of a neural network has been viewed by some as being similar to that of the brain. Neural networks are especially suited to simulating intelligence in pattern detection, association, and classification activities. Financial organizations are now the second-greatest sponsors of research in neural network applications (after the Department of Defense, which in 1989 embarked on a five-year, multimillion-dollar program for neural network research).

4.6.1   How Neural Networks Learn

Neural networks consist of many simple processors, all of which are programmed to perform the same elementary task, for which each uses a small local memory area. An individual processor is referred to as a *processing element* or *PE*. Each has one output but more than one input (see Figure 4.3). Outputs of one PE become inputs to other PEs or outputs of the network. The output can also be fed back as an input to the same PE.

Figure 4.3
A Neural-Processing Element

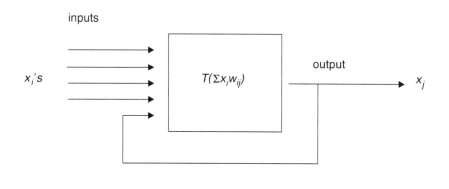

In most neural network paradigms, the actual processing that takes place within each PE — taking a weighted sum of the inputs and calculating an output value that is a function of the sum — is relatively simple. The process is represented as

$$x_j = T\left(\sum_i w_{ij} x_i\right),$$

where x_j is the output of processing element j, w_{ij} is the weighting coefficient of the interconnect link between processing elements i and j, and T is a *transfer* or *activation function*. The most commonly used transfer functions are variations of the S-shaped sigmoid

$$\left(1 - e^{-\sum(\cdot)}\right)^{-1}.$$

However, other functions, including Z-shaped (hard limiting) and threshold detector (flip-flop) are also used in some applications. The PE's local memory stores interconnect weights and parameters used by its transfer function. When many processors are linked, a neural network is created.

Learning takes place through incremental changes in interconnect weight coefficients according to a learning rule. For example, under the *delta rule* for learning, the change in interconnect weight Δw_{ij} is made proportional to the error between the desired output o_j and the actual output x_j:

$$\Delta w_{ij} = ke_j x_i ,$$

where x_i is the level of the input to PE j from PE i, e_j is the error $o_j - x_j$, and k is a constant that determines the learning rate. The delta rule is somewhat analogous to gradient descent, as changes are made that lead to local improvement only. There are about a half-dozen different learning rules in common use.

What mainly distinguishes one neural network from another is the pattern of interconnections among the PEs. There are about twenty different network configurations, about a dozen of which are commonly employed. In most of these, individual networks are combined in layers that operate in synchrony with one another. Normally there is an input layer, output layer, and one or more "hidden" layers. Since the computation that takes place in each PE is relatively simple, and can be done concurrently with that taking place in other PEs in the network, extremely high processing speeds can be achieved. To date, most neural networks have been emulated by software operating on conventional hardware; however, neural processing elements are now becoming implemented on integrated circuit chips, making it possible to dramatically increase processing speeds.

4.6.2   Strengths and Weaknesses

Neural network technology has some advantages over conventional ES approaches in some applications. First of all, since neural networks do not require knowledge to be formalized, they are appropriate for domains in which knowledge is scanty. Second, conventional expert systems map input responses into progressively refined, but linearly separable spaces; neural networks can develop input-output map boundaries that are highly nonlinear (see Figure 4.2). Some types of problems benefit greatly from this capability. Third, although most ES shells permit classification probabilities to be incorporated into rules, these probabilities must ordinarily be explicitly entered; some types of neural networks are able to deduce these probabilities through training. Fourth, it is difficult for auto-learning rule-based ESs to develop rules from historical data when the inputs are highly correlated; neural network-learning paradigms do not suffer from this problem. Finally, the per-case processing time of neural networks can be faster than that of conventional systems, since the network examines all of the information available about a problem at the same time; this facilitates a more highly automated input interface.

On the other hand, neural networks have several weaknesses. One of these is that neural network ESs may identify certain factors as being important for decision making, when these factors are actually irrelevant, or in conflict with traditional theories in the knowledge domain. Since the scope of training is always to some extent limited by economics and time, networks that contradict accepted theory run the risk of lacking generality, or functioning well only on data with a structure similar to that of the training set.

Also, most neural networks cannot guarantee an optimal or completely certain solution to a problem, or sometimes even repeatability with the same input data. Nevertheless, as will be seen in later examples, properly configured and trained neural networks often make, in a statistical sense, consistently good classifications, generalizations, or decisions.

Neural networks can be useful in automating both routine and ad hoc financial analysis tasks (Chithelin 1989). Prototype neural network-based decision aids have been built for the following applications:

- Credit-authorization screening

- Mortgage-risk assessment

- Project management and bidding strategy

- Economic predictions

- Risk rating of exchange-traded fixed-income investments

- Detection of irregularities in security price movements

Other potential applications meriting further research, development, and evaluation are the following:

- Portfolio selection and diversification

- Simulation of market behavior

- Index construction

- Identification of explanatory economic factors
- "Mining" of financial and economic databases

4.7   NEURAL NETWORK APPLICATIONS

The ability of neural networks to classify data with attributes that are highly correlated makes them quite useful for risk-assessment applications. The Nestor Company has used neural networks in the area of mortgage underwriting to make risk-classification decisions based on historical data (Collins, Ghosh and Scofield 1988). Nestor's network is designed to produce predictive risk assessments of mortgage insurance policies. After being trained on previous underwriter judgments, the system produced more consistent classifications than did the company's human underwriters.

The AVCO Corporation applied a neural network to consumer credit scoring. The trained network was reportedly able to increase lending volume by more than 25% over that produced by conventional statistical scoring procedures, without increasing the default rate. Also, the company discovered in field trials that of the 96 individual score items normally used, only 46 were actually needed for making satisfactory assessments of risk.

In risk assessment, which is a generalization problem, a network is expected to correctly predict an output from an input that is not contained in the set of examples that the network was trained with. Dutta and Shekhar (1988) have successfully applied neural network technology to the generalization problem of rating bonds. Their network was able to categorize bonds with a total squared error an order of magnitude smaller than the most competitive conventional approach (multiple regression). Standard ES approaches (e.g., rule-based systems) are difficult to apply successfully to this particular problem, because the domain lacks a well-defined model or theory.

Other applications of neural networks that could be of interest to investment managers include economic forecasting, index construction, portfolio selection, and financial market simulation. Certain types of neural networks are designed to recognize regularities in time series even when the functions are highly nonlinear. Demonstrations for neural network products often include the predicting of stock prices from historical data.

White (1988) employed a neural network approach to search for regularities in returns on IBM stock. The training sample covered a 1000-day period from late 1974 to early 1978. The evaluation periods were the 500 days immediately preceding and following the training period. Although White was unable to reject the efficient market hypothesis using this approach, other researchers have reported favorable results from uncovering subtle price anomalies via neural networks (see Chapter 9).

Theoretically, neural networks could also construct indexes by using individual time series as building blocks, thereby reducing massive data sets to a manageable number of utilitarian figures. The components of the index and their weights would be generated to effectuate the index's intended use; for example, a neural network-generated leading index of interest rates would incorporate weights for individual rate and other components that maximize its predictive power. These weights could be found by training the network with historical data. Analogously to statistical smoothing, network-generated weights would be adaptive, with values that drift over time. Periodically, some components could drop out entirely, to be replaced by others.

This computational approach would be especially useful if it were not certain which economic variables were impacting upon the phenomenon in question. For example, according to Arbitrage Pricing Theory (APT), stock returns are generated by a factor model of some sort. However, there may be hundreds or even thousands of factors to choose from. Neural networks could determine, possibly with a much greater degree of accuracy than conventional statistical techniques, which of these factors were most pervasive for particular stocks.

Another potentially fruitful area for the employment of neural networks is in "database mining" (Hecht-Nielson 1987). Here the object is to discover anomalous trends and correlations among seemingly unrelated data. Given the tremendous amount of private and public financial and economic information available, conventional technology would quickly be overwhelmed by such a task.

In a pioneering paper, Hopfield and Tank (1985) reported that they solved a particularly difficult type of optimization problem, known as the traveling-salesman problem, by using a two-layer neural network. They and other researchers have subsequently experimented with neural networks in solving a variety of optimization problems. Of particular relevance to investment is a neural network methodology developed by Zhao and Mendel (1988) for solving a quadratic programming problem closely related to that of the Markowitz portfolio diversification model (see Chapter 3). Because neural networks potentially have a computational speed many times faster than that of conventional computers, these networks may eventually be used to do dynamic adjustment of portfolio mixes that use thousands of available assets, and to keep the huge covariance matrix updated in real-time.

On a somewhat different track, neural computer technology could be used to revolutionize the design and execution of detailed simulation experiments involving models of economic systems (or physical systems) that comprise numerous, highly diffused elements. For example, the behavior of commodity and security markets may be simulated with realistic complexity; thus, definitive research on the institutional factors and policies affecting market stability could be done using neural computers.

4.8   CONCLUSIONS

The application of knowledge-based systems to portfolio selection and related investment management activities is at a relatively early stage of development, with much of the current work still taking place at the research level. Auto-learning systems have certain advantages over programmed systems; and machine learning, while generally difficult to implement initially, may offer significant benefits when reliable expert knowledge is difficult or impossible to come by, and when pattern recognition capability is important.

To date, the most successful commercial use of knowledge-based systems has been as consultant systems that assist professionals in one or more specific aspects of their work (e.g., the formulation of goals and preferences or the implementation of a particular investment strategy). Preprogrammed personal computer "black box" ESs for security selection, such as AIQ Systems' STOCKEXPERT, are becoming popular for personal investing, and investment recommendations based on these systems' assessments are available over premium-billed 900 telephone numbers.

ENDNOTES

1.   Much of the material in this chapter originally appeared in Trippi (1990).

2. The references preceded by asterisks are reprinted in Trippi and Turban (1990).

REFERENCES[2]

The Athena Group, 1987. Portfolio Management Advisor. *Expert Systems* (February): 54–65.

Bestor, J., 1987. Using Expert Systems to Improve Lenders' Performance During Mergers and Acquisitions. *J. Comm. Bank Lend.* (March): 10–16.

*Braun, H. and Chandler, J., 1987. Predicting Stock Market Behavior Through Rule Induction: An Application of the Learning-From-Example Approach. *Decision Sciences* 18: 415–29.

Chithelin, I., 1989. New Technology Learns Wall Street's Mindset. *Wall Street Comp. Rev.* (June): 19–21.

*Clarkson, G. P., 1963. A Model of the Trust Investment Process. *In Computers and Thought*, ed. E. Feigenbaum and J. Feldman. New York: McGraw Hill.

*Cohen, P. and Lieberman, M., 1983. A Report on Folio: an Expert Assistant for Portfolio Managers. *Proceedings of the International Joint Conference on Artificial Intelligence,* 212–14.

Collins, E., Ghosh, S., and Scofield, C., 1988. An Application of a Multiple Neural Network Learning System to Emulation of Mortgage Underwriting Judgments. *Proceedings of the IEEE International Conference on Neural Networks* (July): II-459–66.

*Dutta, S. and Shekhar, S., 1988. Bond Rating: A Non-Conservative Application of Neural Networks. *Proceedings of the IEEE International Conference on Neural Networks* (July): II-443–50.

*Friedland, J., 1988. The Expert Systems Revolution. *Institutional Investor* (July): 77–90.

*Gerkey, P. and Landerholm, K., 1988. Watchdog Investment Monitoring System. *PC AI* (July–August): 14–17.

Hecht-Nielson, R., 1987. Neurocomputer Applications. *National Computer Conference Proceedings,* 239–44.

*Heuer, S., Koch, U., and Cryer, C., 1988. INVEST: An Expert System for Financial Investments. *IEEE EXPERT* (Summer): 60–8.

Holsapple, C., Whinston, A., and Tam, K., 1987. Inductive Approaches to Acquire Trading Rules. *ES in Business '87 Proceedings*, 103–19.

Hopfield, J., and Tank, D., 1984. Neural Computation of Decisions in Optimization Problems. *Biological Cybernetics 52.*

*Kandt, K., and Yuenger, P., 1988. A Trader's Workstation. *Proceedings, 1988 Annual Meeting, Decision Sciences Institute,* 298–301.

King, D., 1988. Building Computerized Financial Advisors: The User Model and Human Interface. Working Paper, Execucom Systems Corporation.

*Lee, J., and Stohr, E., 1985. Representing Knowledge for Portfolio Management Decision Making. *Proceedings of the Second Conference on Artificial Intelligence.*

*Lee, J. K., Chu, S., and Kim, H., 1989. Intelligent Stock Portfolio Management System. *Expert Systems 6* (April): 74–87.

Lee, J. K., Trippi, R. R., Chu, Sl, and Kim, H., 1990. K-FOLIO: Integrating the Markowitz Model with a Knowledge-Based System, *Journal of Portfolio Management 16* (Fall): 89–93.

*Liang, T. and Chen, K., 1987. Issues in Developing Expert Systems for Program Trading. *ES in Business '87 Proceedings,* 145–59.

Mostert, J., Chandra, M., and Rao, S., 1989. LBOCON Leveraged Buy Out Consultant: An Application of Expert Systems in Finance. *Proceedings, 1989 Annual Meeting, Decision Sciences Institute,* New Orleans.

Newell, A., and Simon, H. A., 1972. *Human Problem Solving.* Englewood Cliffs, NJ: Prentice-Hall.

Rau, L., 1988. Conceptual Information Extraction from Financial News. *Proceedings of the Hawaii International Conference on Systems Science,* 501–9.

Shannon, S., 1985. The "Expert" That Thinks Like an Underwriter. *Management Technology* (February).

Sviokla, J., 1988. Expert Systems and Their Impact on the Firm: The Effects of Planpower Use on the Information-Processing Capacity of the Financial Collaborative. *Proceedings of the Hawaii International Conference on Systems Science,* 791–802.

Trippi, R., 1990. Intelligent Systems for Investment Decision Making. In *Managing Institutional Assets,* ed. F. Fabozzi. New York: Harper & Row.

Trippi, R. and Turban, E., 1990. *Investment Management: Decision Support and Expert Systems.* Boston: Boyd & Fraser Div., Southwestern Publishing Company. Reprint. New York: Van Nostrand Reinhold, 1991.

*Talluru, L. R., and Akgiray, V., 1988. Knowledge Representation for Investment Strategy Selection. *Proceedings of the Hawaii International Conference on Systems Science.*

Talluru, L. R., and Akgiray, V., 1990. Problem Representation in Decision Support Systems: An Illustration from Financial Investments. *Proceedings, 1990 Annual Meeting, Decision Sciences Institute,* San Diego, 481–3.

*White, H., 1988. Economic Prediction Using Neural Networks: The Case of IBM Daily Stock Returns. *Proceedings of the IEEE International Conference on Neural Networks* (July): II-451–8.

Zhao, X., and Mendel, J., 1988. An Artificial Neural Minimum-Variance Estimator. *Proceedings of the IEEE International Conference on Neural Networks* (July): II-499–506.

CHAPTER 5

Portfolio-Selection-System Issues

5.1 EXPERT SYSTEM COMPONENTS

As discussed earlier, artificial intelligence is the branch of information science concerned with enabling computers to imitate human intelligence. The question is, to what degree can a computer be made to imitate the intellectual activities that make a human an expert in an area such as security analysis. To design a knowledge-based system, it is necessary to understand exactly what the required type and level of intelligence is.

As shown in Figure 5.1 (Forsyth 1984 and Waterman 1986), the key elements of a traditional expert system are a knowledge base, an inference engine, explanation capability, and a knowledge acquisition system. The goals of the system are achieved through the effective management of knowledge. If the fields of AI are mapped with the architecture of expert systems, they will have the correspondence summarized in Table 5.1.

Figure 5.1
Typical Expert-System Architecture

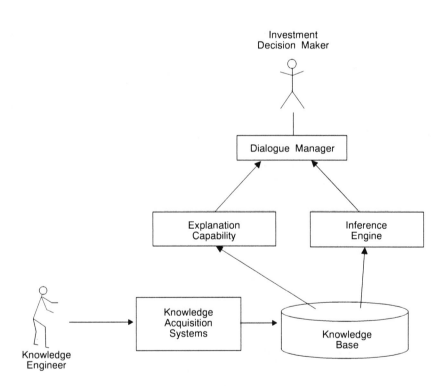

Table 5.1
Relationship between Expert Systems and Artificial Intelligence

Expert System Components	Artificial Intelligence Fields
Knowledge Base	Knowledge Representation
Inference Engine	Reasoning, Logic, Problem Solving
Explanation Capability	Reasoning, Logic, Problem Solving
Knowledge-Acquisition System	Machine Learning
Dialogue Manager	Natural-Language Processing
	Voice Recognition

1. The knowledge representation chosen, for example *rules,* provides the syntax of the specific knowledge base. What most ES developers mean by *knowledge* is a set of certain types of symbolic expressions, in contrast to numeric ones.

2. Reasoning, logical inference, and problem-solving capabilities are normally built into the ES's inference engine. In the AI literature, the term *problem solving* refers to a methodology for *finding paths from initial status to goal status.* Problem-solving techniques include general problem-solver and search algorithms, some of which have been given names (e.g., the A^* algorithm).

3. Explanation synthesis is a type of inference used to justify a certain conclusion and organize the justification information in a form suitable for interpretation by the decision maker.

4. Intelligent editing capability is a virtual necessity for a knowledge-acquisition system. Machine learning is one mechanism for automating knowledge acquisition. Vision may also be used to recognize iconic or visual information during the knowledge-acquisition process.

5. Natural-language processing and voice recognition may be beneficially employed to provide a user-friendly dialogue.

Many expert system researchers agree that AI is a major source for enriching ES; however, AI is not the only source. Investment decision experts also use mathematical programming models for optimization and statistical models for estimation. (Without these decision aids, the ES would imitate a handicapped expert, and produce unsatisfactory results.) In order to choose the appropriate tools, it is necessary to expand the notion of a knowledge base and inference engine. Numerical models may be seen as another type of knowledge representation, and algorithms, such as simplex algorithm to solve linear programming problems, as a means of numerical inference for problem solving. In order to expand and unify the notion of representation and inference, it will be helpful to reinterpret mathematical models from the ES's point of view.

In addition, machine learning and statistical inference are closely related. One of the major goals of statistics is to extract parameters from a large data set; thus, statistical methods such as discriminant and regression analysis could be used as a means of inductive learning.

For these reasons, the architecture of integrating knowledge and mathematical models is an important topic. Chapter 10 of this book will focus on the integration of an optimization problem derived from the Markowitz model with a knowledge base. Before studying the characteristics of ES for investment decisions, however, it will be beneficial to review the terminology and basic concepts of knowledge representation and inference strategies for rule- and frame-based systems.

5.2   RULE-BASED SYSTEMS

Some typical knowledge representation schemes that are used in commercial expert system building tools are rules and frames. The term *frame* can be used interchangeably with the term *object*.

5.2.1   Representation in Rule-based Systems

A rule-based system contains two types of knowledge: rules and facts. A rule is composed of a pair of conditions and actions. Figure 5.2 shows a part of the rule base that can be used as an investment decision aid.

Facts are a collection of assertions and derivations from the rules. A fact base is sometimes called a database. For example, assume the following facts are known about a certain stock:

$$
\begin{aligned}
\text{Industry} &= \text{Electronics} \\
\text{Debt Ratio} &= 80\% \\
\text{Growth Rate} &= 40\%
\end{aligned}
$$

Figure 5.2
Rule Examples

RULE	Rule 10	
IF	Industry	= Electronics
AND	Debt	= Low
AND	Growth	= High
THEN	Grade	= AA or AAA

RULE	Rule 21	
IF	Growth Rate ≥ 30%	
THEN	Growth	= High

RULE	Rule 22	
IF	Growth Rate < 30%	
AND	Growth Rate ≥ 10%	
THEN	Growth	= Medium

RULE	Rule 23	
IF	Growth Rate < 10%	
THEN	Growth	= Low

RULE	Rule 31	
IF	Debt Ratio	≤ 100%
THEN	Debt	= Low

Using the above facts, which could have been retrieved from a simple database, the following facts may be derived according to Rule 21 and Rule 31:

Growth = High
Debt   = Low

It is also possible to derive the following fact according to Rule 10:

Grade = AA or AAA

This sort of fact base may be generated for each consulting session and for each stock.

5.2.2   Inference Strategies

There are two general types of inference strategies: forward chaining and backward chaining. To explain these strategies, the rule base is converted into an acyclic AND/OR digraph (see Figure 5.3). *Digraph* means directed graph, while the arc in the figure indicates the AND relationship.

Forward Chaining Strategy

From the graph, forward chaining begins the reasoning process by asking about the facts at the leaf nodes, such as industry, debt ratio, and growth rate. Once the facts are given, the debt and growth status are derived by tracing the directed nodes. The iteration is continued until a certain conclusion is reached, at which time the inference is ended. The forward chaining strategy is sometimes called a bottom-up strategy or data-driven inference.

Backward Chaining Strategy

A backward chaining strategy starts with a conclusion node such as *Grade = AAA*. To confirm whether an indicated stock satisfies the conclusion or not, the system traces down the directing nodes, eventually reading leaf nodes such as industry, debt ratio, and growth rate, at which point questions are asked. The first of these might be

What is the industry?

If the answer is *Electronics*, more questions will follow, concerning debt ratio and growth rate; these in turn will be followed by additional questions. If the answers to these satisfy the conditions for the current conclusion, the satisfaction of current goal has been confirmed, and the inference process may be stopped; however, if the goal "AAA" is not satisfied, the procedure of searching for satisfaction of next-level goals must be continued in an iterative fashion. Simply showing the rules that are related to the conclusion "Grade = AAA" is often a good source of explanation.

Figure 5.3
An Illustrative AND/OR Digraph

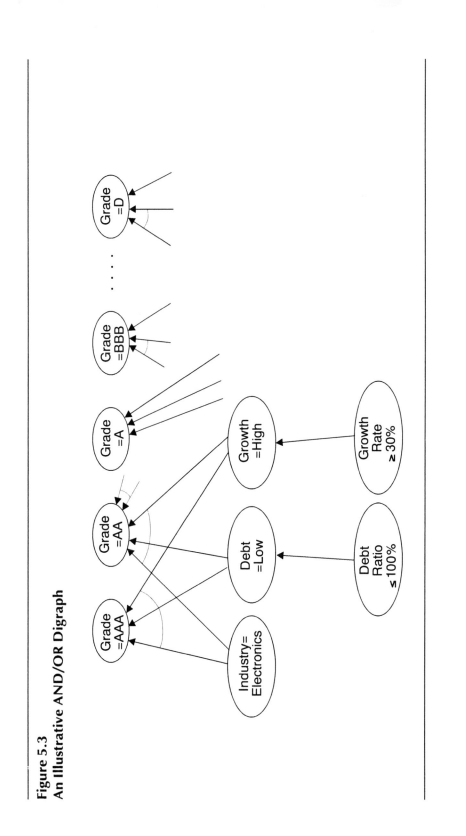

5.3   FRAME-BASED SYSTEMS

Frames are an effective medium for representing the concept of objects, class-instance relationships, and demons (procedures attached to slots, as will be explained later). In a frame, the attributes of an object are repre-sented in *slots* (see Figure 5.4). For instance, in the example frame IBM, there are slots for sales, growth rate, and debt ratio. The value of a slot may be a single value or multiple values in the form of a list. As illus-

Figure 5.4
Structure of Frame-based Representation

Structure of a Frame

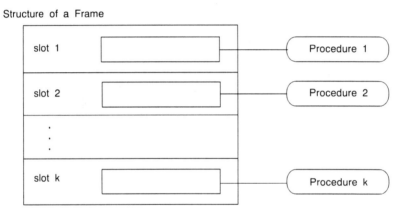

An Example Frame IBM

trated by the sales slot, multiple values may be further specified in the lower-level frame or *facet* attached to the slot.

Frames can be arranged in a hierarchical structure (see Figure 5.5). Hierarchical relationships are an effective means of representing the way in which the linked lower-level frames inherit values from the higher-level frames. Bottom-up summation and averaging can also be managed using the hierarchy. The procedures attached to slots are called demons. The typical roles of demons fall into three categories:

IF-ADDED   : execute the procedure when a value is added to the slot.

IF-REMOVED   : execute the procedure when a value is removed from the slot.

IF-NEEDED   : execute the procedure when the value of the slot is requested.

Figure 5.5
Hierarchical Structure of Frames

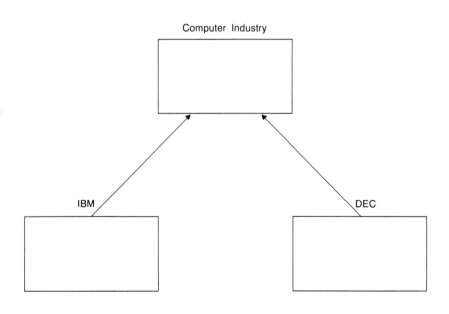

Since frames are just another way of organizing data, the frame base is also called an object-oriented database. Therefore the fact base of a rule-based system may adopt the frame-based representation. Currently, the trend is to integrate frames and rules together in this manner. Most advanced tools in the expert system building tool market belong to this category. Well-known software tools include KEE, ART, Knowledge Craft, NEXPERT Object, Level-5 Object, and UNIK.

5.4   INVESTMENT SUPPORT FEATURES

The following are some distinctive characteristics of the expert systems that support security investment decisions. Each of these will be examined in more detail in later chapters.

5.4.1   Knowledge Representation

Knowledge representation for investment must satisfy the following requirements.

Industry vs. Company Classification

Since information must be kept at both the industry level and the individual company level, it is necessary to distinguish between the class (e.g., industry) and individuals within the class (e.g., particular companies). Classifying criteria such as countries or sectors might also be used as higher-level classes. Frame-based representation makes it possible to handle these features in an efficient manner. The inheritance of industry data by individual companies, as well as the averaging-up and summing-up of individual companies' data into the class, is facilitated by the frame representation. The *exception* representation is also necessary in order to express a situation such as

Good industry except for bad companies in the industry

or

Bad industry except for good companies in the industry

Uncertainty Handling

In the illustrative rules given in Figure 5.2, there exist no uncertainties. In practice, however, it is rare to come to a conclusion with 100% confidence. Therefore, it is desirable that each rule contain information about the *level of confidence*. The same holds true for facts. For example, a company may sell both electronic products and machinery. In this case, the industry classification is not deterministic. Again, estimated values about sales amount and growth rate cannot normally be predicted with 100% confidence. Therefore, facts also need to contain confidence-level information. (Uncertainty issues will be dealt with further in Chapters 6 and 7.)

Multiple Sources of Knowledge

Knowledge may be acquired from several sources. At the minimum, a commonly shared expert's knowledge must be distinguished from each individual investor's knowledge and preferences. To accommodate diverse sources of knowledge, the syntax of the knowledge should be uniform, and conflicting knowledge from different sources should be systematically resolvable. (See Chapter 8.)

Integration with Optimization

Since an optimization model such as the Markowitz model can be used as a tool in portfolio decision making, integration of knowledge with the appropriate optimization model should be attempted. (See Chapter 10.)

Integration with a Database

Since historical data about stock prices, trading volumes, and financial statements can be effectively maintained in a traditional database such as a flat-file or relational database, integration of the ES with such a database is essential. (See Chapters 8 and 11.)

5.4.2   Inference and Explanation

In order to identify the ES inference and explanation capabilities required, it is necessary to define the dialogue capability appropriate to investment. Typical dialogues might be the following.

Individual Stock Evaluation. Each individual stock may be evaluated and classed into one of the following ten grades: AAA, AA, A, BBB, BB, B, CCC, CC, C, or D. Grading stocks is essentially a classification problem involving the concepts of value discussed in Chapters 2 and 3. Either a forward- or backward-chaining inference strategy may be adopted; however, since some numeric factors are compensatory in grading, these factors may have to be combined through a weighted linear combination scheme. Thus, the inference method described in this book is not exactly the same as the typical forward- and backward-chaining strategies. (See Chapter 8.)

Industry-Level Evaluation. Stocks in an industry may be evaluated with the same grading scheme that is used for individual stock evaluation.

Criteria-based Evaluation. The grade of a group of stocks that satisfy certain criteria may be requested by the user. If the questioned criterion is exactly the same as that in a rule already available, the grade can be directly retrieved from the conclusion part of the rule. If the criterion is not exactly the same, however, a conclusion should be synthesized through a case-based reasoning process.

Ordering Stocks by Grade. This is a simple sorting of stocks that have already been evaluated.

Explanation Generation. The rules associated with a certain conclusion should be organized so as to explain the reasons why a stock has been evaluated in a certain way. After examining the reasons, the decision maker may wish to change the weight of some reasons interactively. Therefore, there is a need to support interactive sensitivity analysis from the explanation screen.

Dynamic Decision Making. A sequence of dynamic selling/buying decisions for a stock may be necessary for some investment strategies.

5.4.3   Knowledge Acquisition and Maintenance

In order to accommodate the changing security market environment, a user-friendly knowledge-editing and machine-learning process should be supported.

Knowledge-Editing Aids

Classifying knowledge categories is useful for deciding the relative location of frames to be added, updated, or deleted.

Meta-Knowledge Guide

In order to determine how frequently a particular type of knowledge needs to be updated, the expected life span of each knowledge component should be maintained. The bits of knowledge that exhaust their life spans each day can be displayed so that their authors can review the knowledge to decide whether to delete, modify, or extend its life span. The names of these authors should also be kept so that the knowledge of each individual author can be accessed while maintaining an appropriate level of security protection.

Machine Learning

Inductive learning schemes, such as ID3 and neural networks, can be used to generate rules from instances of historical investment data. For example, when charts are used to search for buy or sell cues, a facility for automatic recognition of patterns and synthesis of rules from those patterns is necessary. (See Chapter 9.)

5.4.4   System Architecture

The expert system known as K-FOLIO effectively handles many of the issues raised in this chapter. Its overall architecture is shown in Figure 5.6. The K-FOLIO system will be used to illustrate many of the concepts discussed in subsequent chapters.

Figure 5.6
Architecture of K-FOLIO

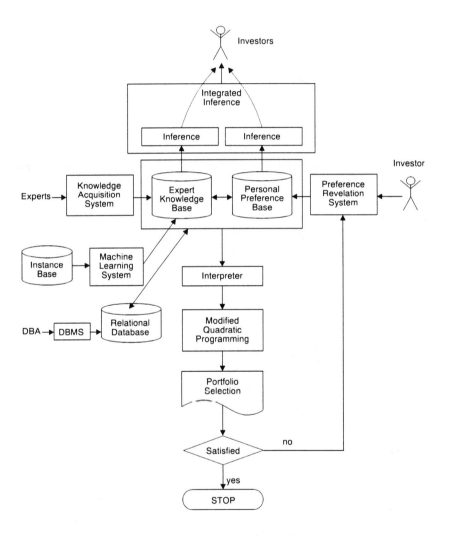

REFERENCES

Forsyth, R., ed., 1984. *Expert Systems: Principles and Case Studies.* Chapman Hall Computing.

Waterman, D. A., 1986. *A Guide to Expert Systems.* Addison Wesley.

CHAPTER 6

Knowledge Representation and Inference

6.1   INTRODUCTION

This chapter will describe how K-FOLIO represents knowledge, evaluates individual stocks, and explains the reasons for its actions. The structure of the knowledge base and inference procedure of K-FOLIO is shown in Figure 6.1 (Lee, Chu, and Kim 1989). Three key components of K-FOLIO's knowledge system are the rule base, the database, and an inference procedure.

There are three rule bases; these contain company-based, industry-based, and attribute-based rules. Rules incorporate knowledge into the system using a consistent representational format.

There are also three databases: a company-based relational database, an industry-based relational database, and a working memory base. The working memory base stores list-type data and derived statements from rules in an unstructured fashion.

The inference procedure begins with a matching of each of the rule bases with its own relevant databases, which generates a rule set for each individual company and industry. The rule set is called a *conflict set* because each rule may support a different conclusion. The conflict set is used to evaluate stocks and synthesize explanations.

6.2   THE RULE BASE

6.2.1   Syntax of Rules

The syntax of rules is shown in Figure 6.2. A rule has the reserved words RULE, CREDIBILITY (CR), IF, AND, OR, GRADE, EXCEPT, THEN, and BECAUSE, plus arithmetic operators. CR stands for the credibility of the rule as a percentage between 0 and 100.

6.2.2   Example Rules

Examples of rules appear in Figure 6.3. Note the following:

1.   RULE is followed by the rule name.

2.   CR stands for the credibility of a rule, expressed as a percent.

Figure 6.1
Knowledge Management Subsystem

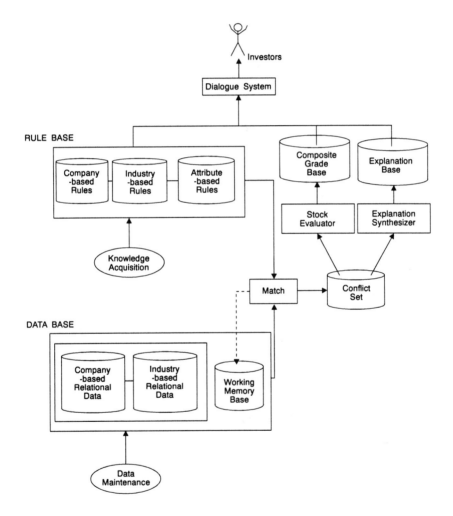

Figure 6.2
Overall Syntax of Rules

```
RULE        rulename
CREDIBILITY = percentage
IF          statement A
(AND        statement B)
(OR         statement C)

        . . .

THEN        statement zz
            GRADE = a grade
            (BECAUSE statement)
            (EXCEPT statement)


Legend
Capital letters : reserved words
( ) : optional statement
```

3. The conditional statements are organized in AND and OR relationships.

4. THEN statements conclude with a GRADE such as the ones in rules 10, 12, and 13; or a statement, such as the one in Rule 11.

5. An EXCEPT statement, such as the one in Rule 12, excludes a company even if the company satisfies the conditions.

6. A BECAUSE statement, such as the one in Rule 10, explains why a stock is given a certain grade.

Rule 10 is a company-based rule; Rule 12 is an industry- and attribute-based rule; and Rules 11 and 13 are attribute-based rules.

6.3   THE DATABASE

6.3.1   Relational Database Examples

Examples of relational databases are shown in Figures 6.4 and 6.5. The company-based relational database in Figure 6.4 lists the company

Figure 6.3
Example Rules

RULE	rule 10
CR =	0.7
IF	Company = ABC
THEN	GRADE = A
	BECAUSE The company ABC has developed a new compact disc player in July 1991.

RULE	rule 11
CR =	0.6
IF	Major Market = Overseas
AND	Annual Sales Growth Rate ≥ 50%
AND	The ratio of indirect and direct financing cost ≥ 1.2
THEN	Issuing CB in the foreign financial market is expected

RULE	rule 12
CR =	0.6
IF	Industry = Electronics
AND	Issuing CB in the foreign financial market is expected
THEN	GRADE = AA
	EXCEPT Company = KK

RULE	rule 13
CR =	0.6
IF	P/E Ratio ≥ 10
AND	Debt Ratio ≥ 200%
THEN	GRADE = C

name, industry, major market, price-earning ratio, annual sales growth rate, debt ratio, fixed ratio, sales and amount of exports, and so on. The industry-based relational database includes industry-level information such as preferential tax advantages and stage of life cycle.

Figure 6.4
Company-based Relational Database

Company	Industry	Major Market	P/E Ratio	Annual Sales Growth Rate	Debt Ratio	Fixed Ratio	Sales	Amount of Exports
ABC	Electronics	Overseas	15.0	90%	500%	450%	60 million	40 million
XYZ	Electronics	Domestic	8.0	60%	400%	300%	120 million	50 million

Figure 6.5
Industry-based Relational Database

Industry	Tax Benefits	Stage of Life Cycle
Electronics	Preferable	Growth
Shipbuilding	Not Preferable	Decline

6.3.2   Inheritance, Average-Up, and Sum-Up

Between the industry database and company database, the principles of inheritance, average-up, and sum-up will apply. The attributes of an industry can be inherited by default to the companies that belong to that industry, and the attributes of companies can be averaged and summed up for the industry. (See Figure 6.6.)

As shown in Figure 6.6, the attributes of the electronics industry — TaxBenefit and Stage of Life Cycle — are inherited to all companies in the industry, except for those that have a prespecified value (such as "no preferences" in the Tax Benefit column of company ABC). On the other hand, some average values of attributes of companies, such as the average annual sales growth rate, can be used for the industry. In the same way, the total amount of exports can also be used for the industry.

These derivations can be invoked by the following declarations in the data definition section.

TITLE	INDUSTRY
FATHER	NONE
CHILD	COMPANY
INHERIT	Tax Benefit, Stage of Life Cycle

TITLE	COMPANY
FATHER	INDUSTRY
CHILD	NONE
AVERAGE-UP	Annual Sales Growth Rate
SUM-UP	Amount of Exports

6.3.3   Working Memory

Working memory may be inserted directly into the working memory base, but most working memory will be generated as intermediate outcomes of the matching process (see Figure 6.7).

In Figure 6.7, four facts about company ABC are given:

Industry = Electronics
Major Market = Overseas
Annual Sales Growth Rate = 60%
Ratio of Indirect and Direct Financing Cost = 1.3

Figure 6.6
Inheritance, Average-Up and Sum-Up

Industry-based Database

Industry	Tax Benefit	Stage of Life Cycle	Average Annual Sales Growth Rate	Total Amount of Exports
Electronics	Preferable	Growth	75%	90 million
Shipbuilding	Not Preferable	Decline		

Company-based Database

Company	Industry	Major Market	P/E Ratio	Annual Sales Growth Rate	Amount of Exports	Tax Benefits	Stage of Life Cycle
ABC	Electronics	Overseas	15.0	90%	40 million	Not Preferable	Growth
XYZ	Electronics	Domestic	8.0	60%	50 million	Preferable	Growth

Debt Ratio	Fixed Ratio	Sales
500%	450%	60 million
400%	300%	120 million

INHERITANCE

AVERAGE-UP

SUM-UP

Figure 6.7
Generated Working Memory in the Matching Process

A Matched Rule

RULE   rule 11
IF   Major Market = Overseas
AND   Annual Sales Growth Rate ≥ 50%
AND   The ratio of indirect and direct financing cost ≥ 1.2

THEN | Issuing CB in the foreign financial market is expected

←insert

Working memory of
DEF company

Working memory of ABC company

Industry = Electronics
Major Market = Overseas
Annual Sales Growth Rate = 60%
Ratio of Indirect and Direct Financing Cost = 1.3

Issuing CB in the foreign financial market is expected

Since the currently known facts satisfy the conditions of Rule 11, the conclusion is derived and added to the working memory of company ABC. Other companies, such as company DEF, will also include the derived statement.

If the conclusion of the matched rule is a GRADE statement, however, the conclusion will not be included in the working memory; rules with GRADE statements are goal rules, which do not have any succeeding rules. The matching process will stop if all the matched rules have GRADE statements.

6.4   SECURITY INFERENCE

The security inference procedure comprises three steps: (1) conflict-set generation, (2) composite-grade generation, and (3) explanation synthesis.

6.4.1   Conflict-Set Generation

The conflict set consists of multiple GRADE-type rules matched for a company or industry. As shown in Figure 6.8, different rules support different grades.

6.4.2   Composite-Grade Generation

In order to resolve the conflicts in the conflict set, it is necessary to use the grades and CR in the rules to compute a composite grade. To permit

---

Figure 6.8
Rules in Conflict Set of Company ABC

RULE	rule 10
CR =	0.7
IF	Company = ABC
THEN	GRADE = A
	BECAUSE The company ABC has developed a new compact disc player in July.

RULE	rule 12
CR =	0.6
IF	Industry = Electronics
AND	Issuing CB in the foreign financial market is expected
THEN	GRADE = AA

RULE	rule 13
CR =	0.6
IF	P/E Ratio $\geq$ 10
AND	Debt Ratio $\geq$ 200%
THEN	GRADE = C

numeric computation, the grades are transformed into numbers between −1 and +1. (The mapping values are shown in Table 6.1.)

The rules in the conflict set are then categorized into two groups, one comprised of rules that support positive evidence, and the other of rules that support negative evidence. If the evidence conflicts, the positive and negative evidence should be compensatory to one another. To operationalize this idea, one may adopt a composition scheme in which credibility levels are used as weighting factors to generate composite subgrades; the subgrades are then combined by the formula shown in Table 6.1.

Table 6.1
Grades and Corresponding Real Numbers

Grade	Real number	Median	Description
AAA	$0.8 < n \leq 1.0$	0.9	Highly Recommended
AA	$0.6 < n \leq 0.8$	0.7	↑
A	$0.4 < n \leq 0.6$	0.5	
BBB	$0.2 < n \leq 0.4$	0.3	
BB	$0.0 < n \leq 0.2$	0.1	Unknown
B	$-0.2 < n \leq 0.0$	−0.1	
CCC	$-0.4 < n \leq -0.2$	−0.3	
CC	$-0.6 < n \leq -0.4$	−0.5	↓
C	$-0.8 < n \leq -0.6$	−0.7	
D	$-1.0 \leq n \leq -0.8$	−0.9	Highly Prohibited

The composite stock grading model employs the following notation:

G_i = composite grade of stock i based on all rules

G_i^+ = composite grade of stock i based on rules with positive grades

G_i^- = composite grade of stock i based on rules with negative grades

g_r^+ = positive grade of stock i by rule r

g_r^- = negative grade of stock i by rule r

C_r = credibility of rule r

P = rule set with positive grade for stock i

N = rule set with negative grade for stock i

p = number of rules in set P

n = number of rules in set N.

Positive and negative subgrades are given by

$$G_i^+ = \sum_{r \in P} C_r g_r^+ - \sum_{\substack{s < t \\ s,t \in P}} (C_s g_s^+)(C_t g_t^+) + \dots$$

$$+ (-1)^{p+1} \prod_{r \in P} C_r g_r^+$$

and

$$G_i^- = \sum_{r \in N} C_r g_r^- + \sum_{\substack{s < t \\ s,t \in N}} (C_s g_s^-)(C_t g_t^-) + \dots$$

$$+ \prod_{r \in N} C_r g_r^-$$

These are combined into the composite grade of stock i by

$$G_i = \frac{G_i^+ + G_i^-}{1 - \min\{|G_i^+|, |G_i^-|\}}.$$

For example, consider the rules associated with company ABC in Figure 6.8:

$$G_{ABC}^+ = (0.6 \times 0.7 + 0.7 \times 0.5) - (0.6 \times 0.7 \times 0.7 \times 0.5) = 0.623$$

$$G_{ABC}^- = 0.6 \times (-0.7) = -0.42$$

and

$$G_{ABC} = \frac{0.623 - 0.42}{1 - 0.42} = 0.35.$$

ABC stock is evaluated as 0.35, which can also be converted into the grade *BBB*. The composite grade is stored in the composite grade base.

Two special types of preemptive grades are GRADE = *** and GRADE = *ZZZ*. If a GRADE = *** exists in the conflict set, the stock will be evaluated as *AAA* regardless of which grades may exist in other rules. In the same way, the grade *ZZZ* will set the stock to the *D* grade preemptively.

Formula 6.1 has the following desirable properties:

1. $0 \leq G_i^+ \leq 1.$

2. $-1 \leq G_i^- \leq 0.$

3. $-1 \leq G_i \leq 1.$

4. Positive grades and negative grades are mutually compensatory.

5. The mutual compensation is symmetric.

6.4.3   Explanation Synthesis

The conflict set can also be used to generate explanations of why stocks are evaluated in a certain way (see Figure 6.9). An explanation is synthesized using the IF and BECAUSE statements in the conflict set. This explanation may be grouped into positive reasons and negative reasons, and the reasons in each group are ordered by the level of GRADE. The reasons are stored in the explanation base.

If users want to see the reasons for statements made in the explanation, they may select a statement and ask why. For example, the reasoning behind the statement "Issuing Convertible Bond in the foreign financial market is expected" can be determined by using the associated rules shown in Figure 6.10.

6.5   Dialogues

By using the composite grade base, the explanation base, the rule bases, and the databases, K-FOLIO can support four types of dialogue. The

Figure 6.9
Process of Explanation Synthesis

Rules of Conflict Set

RULE	rule 10
CR =	0.7
IF	Company = ABC
THEN	GRADE A
	BECAUSE the company ABC has developed a new compact disc player in July 1991.

RULE	rule 12
CR =	0.6
IF	Industry = Electronics
AND	Issuing CB in the foreign financial market is expected
THEN	GRADE = AA

RULE	rule 13
CR =	0.6
IF	P/E Ratio ≥ 10
AND	Debt Ratio ≥ 200%
THEN	GRADE = C

ABC company
Recommendation Level = BBB

Explanation

Positive Reasons

1. Industry = Electronics
2. Issuing CB in the foreign financial market is expected.
3. The company ABC has developed a new compact disc player in July 1991.

Negative Reasons

1. P/E Ratio = 15 is greater than 10
2. Debt Ratio = 300% is greater than 200%

Figure 6.10
Example of the "WHY" Statement

```
┌──────────────────────────────────────────────────────────┐
│        Issuing CB in the foreign financial market is expected │
└──────────────────────────────────────────────────────────┘
```

WHY

According to the rule

```
┌──────────────────────────────────────────────────────────┐
│  RULE    rule 11                                           │
│                                                            │
│  IF      ┌─────────────────────────────────────┐          │
│          │ Major market = Overseas             │          │
│  AND     Annual Sales Growth Rate ≥ 50%                    │
│  AND     The ratio of indirect and direct financing cost ≥ 1.2 │
│  THEN    Issuing CB in the foreign financial market is expected │
└──────────────────────────────────────────────────────────┘
```

WHY

According to the rule

```
┌──────────────────────────────────────────────────────────┐
│  RULE    rule 8                                            │
│  IF      Amount of Exports > Domestic Sales               │
│  THEN    Major market = Overseas                          │
└──────────────────────────────────────────────────────────┘
```

first of these is an individual company-based dialogue, which helps users to obtain recommendation levels for specific stocks, as well as the reasons why the stocks are recommended. The second dialogue is an industry-based one that is similar to the dialogue described for an individual company. The third dialogue is a criteria-based one whose questions are a combination of various attributes. The fourth dialogue is a grade-based one that is performed by using the composite-grade base. Users may select each type of dialogue from a menu; they may also gain supplementary access to the database for a company and an industry at any given moment.

6.5.1   Company-based Dialogue

A typical dialogue with user responses underlined is shown in Figure 6.11. The dialogue in Figure 6.11 is generated from the composite-grade base and explanation base for company HHH Motors. (Note that the reason inherited from the automobile industry is also included.) If decision makers do not agree with the explanations, they may modify the GRADE and CR as they think appropriate. The system will then interactively recompute the composite grade in accordance with the changes. Personal modifications are local and do not change the values in the common conflict set.

6.5.2   Industry-based Dialogue

The dialogue for an industry is similar to that for an individual stock. In industry-level inference, the average-up and sum-up features are utilized. A special property of industry-based dialogue is the fact that a threshold for exceptionally recommended companies and exceptionally prohibited companies can be denoted by using *except* statements.

6.5.3   Criteria-based Dialogue

Consider the following question, asked by criteria:

IF   annual sales growth rate $\geq 40\%$
AND   debt ratio $\leq 200\%$

The criteria are matched with the conditional parts of the rules in the rule base. If a matching rule exists, that rule will be displayed. For instance,

CR =   0.9
IF   Annual Sales Growth Rate $\geq 35\%$

Figure 6.11
Example of Company-based Dialogue

Type the company name

<u>HHH Motors</u>

Grade of HHH Motors = A

Explanation

   Positive Reasons

      (1)   GRADE = AA with CR = 0.9
            BECAUSE: New model of HHH motors company was
            recorded as one of the most favorable cars
            in the U.S. market.

      (2)   GRADE = A with CR = 0.7 for Automobile Industry

   Negative Reasons

      (1)   GRADE = D with CR = 0.6 for P/E Ratio = 20 is greater
            than 15

AND   Debt Ratio ≤ 200%
THEN GRADE = A

Note that the questioned annual sales growth rate (40%) is larger than the one in the matched rule (35%). We can therefore conclude that the questioned criteria can "at least" satisfy GRADE = A. In general, questions by criteria belong to one of four cases (see Figure 6.12):

   a.   The questioned criteria are stricter than the condition of the matched rule.

   b.   The questioned criteria are looser than the condition of the matched rule.

Figure 6.12
Relationships between Questions and Rules

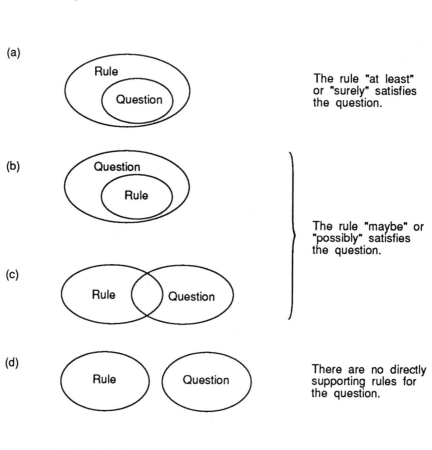

(a)

Rule

Question

The rule "at least" or "surely" satisfies the question.

(b)

Question

Rule

The rule "maybe" or "possibly" satisfies the question.

(c)

Rule   Question

(d)

Rule   Question

There are no directly supporting rules for the question.

---

c. Only a portion of the questioned criteria can be matched with rules.

d. There is no directly matching rule.

For case (a), the rule "at least" or "surely" satisfies the question. For cases (b) and (c), however, it is necessary to conclude with the qualification "maybe" or "possibly." Case-based reasoning techniques may be applied if multiple similar rules exist. In this case, a scheme similar to the composite-grade computation formula discussed in Section 6.4.2

may be applied. If no corresponding rule, such as (d), exists, the questioned grade cannot be answered directly.

Another indirect approach for criteria-based questions is to retrieve the companies that satisfy the criteria and compute the average grade of these companies, which may take an enormous amount of effort. For cases (b), (c), and (d), however, the indirect method may be used as a supplement.

6.5.4   Grade-based Dialogue

When the user simply asks about stocks with a certain grade, AAA for example, the system displays all stocks with that grade. The composite-grade base can support this kind of dialogue.

6.6   CONCLUSIONS

A number of steps are involved in constructing, manipulating, and evaluating rules to arrive at a set of reliable, consistent, and mutually supporting rules. This process is referred to as *rule synergy.*

REFERENCES

Lee, J. K., Chu, S., and Kim, H., 1989. Intelligent Stock Portfolio Management System. *Expert Systems* 6 (April): 74–87.

CHAPTER 7

Handling Investment Uncertainties

7.1   INTRODUCTION

Within the AI literature, there are several methods for handling uncertainty, all of which can be classified as either *numeric* or *nonnumeric.* Numeric methods include *probability theory, possibility theory,* and *evidence theory.* Nonnumeric methods include *nonmonotonic reasoning* and those based on the *theory of endorsement* (Kanal and Lemmer 1986). The methods most applicable to investment decision making are *Bayesian theory* and *certainty factors* in probability theory; *fuzzy logic* in possibility theory; and nonmonotonic reasoning. Through the use of simple investment examples, each of these approaches will be explained in this chapter.

7.2   THE BAYESIAN APPROACH

7.2.1   Definitions and Formulas

In order to demonstrate how Bayesian theory can be applied to investment decision making, it will be helpful to review *Bayes' Theorem* by using the following notation (Naylor 1984):

H : Hypothesis H

H' : Hypothesis "Not H"

E : Evidence E

E' : Evidence "Not E"

$P(H)$　　　: Prior Probability to conclude the hypothesis H

$P(H|E)$　　: Posterior Probability to conclude the hypothesis H with the evidence E

$P(H \cap E)$　: Joint Probability of occurrence of hypothesis H and evidence E

By the definition of conditional probability,

$$P(H|E) = P(H \cap E) / P(E) \tag{7.1}$$

$$P(E \cap H) = P(E|H) P(H). \tag{7.2}$$

By substituting (7.2) into (7.1),

$$P(H \mid E) = P(E \mid H) \, P(H) \, / \, P(E) \tag{7.3}$$

is obtained. Since

$$P(E) = P(E \mid H) \, P(H) + P(E \mid H') \, P(H')$$

and

$$P(H') = 1 - P(H),$$

equation (7.3) can be transformed into

$$P(H \mid E) = P(E \mid H) \, P(H) \, / \, [P(E \mid H) \, P(H) + P(E \mid H') \, (1 - P(H))]. \tag{7.4}$$

By using equation (7.4), it is possible to compute the posterior probability of satisfying the hypothesis H with the given evidence from the available probabilistic data $P(E \mid H)$, $P(E \mid H')$, and $P(H)$.

The computation of (7.4) can be operationalized by utilizing the notions of *odds* and *likelihood ratio*. By definition, the odds $O(H)$ and $O(H \mid E)$ can be expressed as the following:

$$O(H) \quad = P(H) \, / \, [1 - P(H)] \tag{7.5}$$

$$O(H \mid E) = P(H \mid E) \, / \, [1 - P(H \mid E)]. \tag{7.6}$$

Equation (7.6) can be rewritten as

$$O(H \mid E) = [P(E \mid H) \, / \, P(E \mid H')] \, O(H). \tag{7.7}$$

If the likelihood ratio $LR(H \mid E)$ is defined as

$$LR(H \mid E) = P(E \mid H) \, / \, P(E \mid H'), \tag{7.8}$$

(7.7) becomes

$$O(H \mid E) = LR(H \mid E) \, O(H). \tag{7.9}$$

According to equation (7.9), posterior odds can be computed as the product of $O(H)$ and $LR(H\,|\,E)$. Thus, formula (7.9) can be adopted to compute the effect of evidence.

7.2.2   An Illustrative Example

The above formulas can now be used in making an investment decision. Consider the following data:

Example 7.1

Industry	Yield		Total
	High (≥ 30%)	Low (<30%)	
Electronics	40	10	50
Other	50	100	150
Total	90	110	200

This two-dimensional frequency table is created from information about 200 stocks.

Hypothesis H = High in Yield
Hypothesis H' = Low in Yield
Evidence E = Electronics Industry
Evidence E' = Not Electronics Industry

If there is no information about a stock, yield can be estimated from the prior probability by

$P(\text{High})= 90/200 = 0.45$
$P(\text{Low}) = 1-P(\text{High}) = 0.55.$

If the industry to which a stock belongs is known, formula (7.9) may be utilized. A prior odds $O(\text{High})$ is computed as

$$O(\text{High}) = P(\text{High}) / [1-P(\text{High})]$$
$$= (90/200) / [1-90/200]$$
$$= 0.8181.$$

The likelihood ratio is

$$LR(\text{High} \mid \text{Electronics}) = P(\text{Electronics} \mid \text{High}) / P(\text{Electronics} \mid \text{Low})$$
$$= (40/90) / (10/110)$$
$$= 4.888;$$

therefore, from formula (7.9),

$$O(\text{High} \mid \text{Electronics}) = LR(\text{High} \mid \text{Electronics}) \, O(\text{High})$$
$$= (0.8181) (4.888)$$
$$= 3.996.$$

Converting to the posterior probability form yields

$$P(\text{High} \mid \text{Electronics}) = 3.996 / (1 + 3.996)$$
$$= 0.8006.$$

Thus, from the evidence that the stock belongs to the electronics industry, the probability of obtaining a yield greater than 30 percent increases from .45 to .80.

Assuming that there is additional evidence about whether the company has either an export-oriented or domestic-oriented market, the frequency table for the market might look like this:

Market	Yield		Total
	High (≥ 30%)	Low (<30%)	
Export	50	30	80
Domestic	40	80	120
Total	90	110	200

In the same way, the posterior probability can be computed as

$$LR(\text{High} \mid \text{Export}) = P(\text{Export} \mid \text{High}) / P(\text{Export} \mid \text{Low})$$
$$= (50/90) / (30/100)$$
$$= 2.037.$$

Thus,

$$O(\text{High} \mid \text{Electronics, Export})$$
$$= LR \ (\text{High} \mid \text{Export}) \ LR(\text{High} \mid \text{Electronics}) \ O(\text{High})$$
$$= LR \ (\text{High} \mid \text{Export}) \ O(\text{High} \mid \text{Electronics})$$
$$= (2.037) \ (3.996)$$
$$= 8.14,$$

and

$$P(\text{High} \mid \text{Electronics, Export}) = 0.8907.$$

With the possession of two pieces of evidence, the industry and the major market, the probability of receiving a higher yield has increased from 0.45 to 0.8907.

7.2.3   Handling Uncertain Evidence

Thus far, it has been assumed that the evidence is known with certainty, but this may not be true in many cases. For instance, in Example 7.1 it was assumed that companies can be dichotomized according to industry or market criteria; in reality, such characterizations are often a question of degree. A company may produce 60 percent of its products for the electronics industry and sell 50 percent of the total amount to foreign markets.

One way to accommodate uncertain evidence is to apply an interpolation method. As shown in Figure 7.1, the probabilities $[P(H \mid E)$, $P(H)$, $P(H \mid E')]$ may be mapped to $[-1, 0, 1]$. If the position of the evidence on the $[-1, 0, 1]$ scale is known, its corresponding probability can be linearly interpolated.

Figure 7.1
Interpolation Method

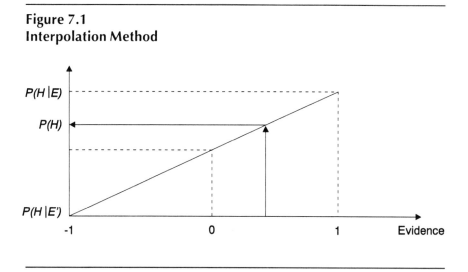

Example 7.2

If a company produces 100 percent of its products for the electronics industry $Ev = 1$; if the company sells no electronics products, $Ev = -1$. If a company sells electronics products at the average proportion of all electronics products relative to the GNP (e.g., 30 percent, the best guess in the absence of industry-specific information), the normalized value of Ev is zero. Assuming that the company produces 60 percent of its products for the electronics industry, the evidence can be normalized as

$$Ev(\text{Electronics}) = (60 - 30) / (100 - 30) = .43;$$

therefore,

$$P(\text{High} \mid Ev(\text{Electronics}) = .43)$$
$$= P(\text{High}) + [P(\text{High} \mid \text{Electronics}) - P(\text{High})] \, Ev(\text{Electronics})$$
$$= 0.45 + (0.80 - 0.45)(0.43)$$
$$= 0.60.$$

Note that the posterior probability is attenuated from .80 to .60 because of the uncertainty of the evidence (see Figure 7.2).

Figure 7.2
An Example of Interpolation

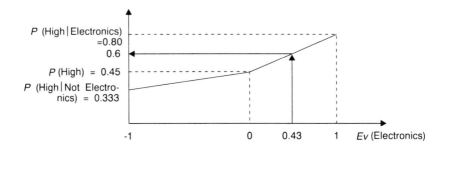

Again, assuming that the normalized evidence of export is

$$Ev(\text{Export}) = .5,$$

the attenuated posterior probability with both pieces of evidence is

$$P(\text{High} \mid Ev(\text{Electronics}) = 0.43, Ev(\text{Export}) = 0.5)$$

$$= P(\text{High}) + [P(\text{High} \mid \text{Electronics}) - P(\text{High})]\, Ev(\text{Electronics})$$

$$+ [P(\text{High} \mid \text{Electronics, Export}) - P(\text{High} \mid \text{Electronics})]\, Ev(\text{Export})$$

$$= 0.45 + (0.80 - 0.45)\,(0.43) + (0.89 - 0.80)\,(0.5)$$

$$= 0.645.$$

7.2.4   Handling More Than Two Levels of Hypotheses

Thus far, stocks have been classified into two classes. Stocks may be classified into more than two classes (e.g., class A, B, C, and D), by straightforwardly extending equations (7.1) through (7.4) into equation

(7.10) below, in which $P(H_i | E)$ denotes the probability of satisfying hypothesis H_i

$$P(H_i | E) = [P(E | H_i) \, P(H_i)] / [\sum_i P(E | H_i) \, P(H_i)]. \qquad (7.10)$$

7.3   INFERENCE STRATEGY IN THE BAYESIAN APPROACH

The simplest strategy involving multiple evidence is to use all of the evidence without considering the sequence of application; however, this strategy in inefficient, because some evidence will, in retrospect, be deemed to have made no contribution at all. Thus, it is desirable to order ·as efficiently as possible the sequence of applying evidence. It is also necessary to set inference-stopping conditions.

7.3.1   The Sequence of Applying Evidence

The sequence in which evidence is applied becomes particularly important when the expert system is being used interactively. Three useful sequencing strategies are random ordering, ordering by importance, and the rule-value approach.

Random Ordering

The chief advantage of random ordering is that it is simple. On the other hand, this method may force the decision maker to deal with trivial evidence.

Ordering by Importance

Because of their previous experience, investors or investment experts may have a good idea of the relative importance of various bits of evidence. They may then order the evidence accordingly.

Rule-Value Approach

When time is short and the availability of computing resources abundant, it may be prudent to apply the rule-value approach, which orders according to the value of evidence by using

$$RV_j = \sum_i |P(H_i|E_j) - P(H_i|E_j')|$$

(7.11)

for evidence E_j. Formula (7.11) represents the sum of posterior probability changes that may occur as a result of knowing whether the evidence E_j is true or false. The system can find evidence such that

$$RV_k = \min_j [RV_j, j = 1,...,n].$$

Formula (7.11) may be modified to sum of squares instead of absolute differences. Weights may also be applied to hypotheses. The major disadvantage of the rule-value approach is its computational burden.

7.3.2   Stopping Rules

The following factors may be applied to set a stopping rule:

M_U : an upper threshold of satisfactory probability

M_L : a lower threshold of unsatisfactory probability

$P(MAX)$: maximum probability with all remaining evidence positive

$P(MIN)$: maximum probability with all remaining evidence negative.

It is reasonable to stop when any of the following conditions are satisfied:

1.   If there is no more evidence left,

compare the $P(H_i|E_j, j = 1, \ldots, n)$, and

choose H_i with $\max_i P(H_i|E_j, j = 1, \ldots, n)$.

2.   If $P(MIN)$ of $H_k > P(MAX)$ of all H_i, $i \neq k$,

the hypothesis H_k is the best alternative.

3.   If $P(MIN)$ of $H_k > M_U$, the hypothesis H_k is satisfied.

It is reasonable to eliminate or prune hypotheses that satisfy the following conditions:

4.   If $P(\text{MAX})$ of $H_k < P(\text{MIN})$ of all H_i, $i \neq k$,

the hypothesis H_k is hopeless.

5.   If $P(\text{MAX})$ of $H_k < M_L$,

the hypothesis H_k is too hopeless to continue.

If none of the conditions (1) to (5) are satisfied, it is necessary to continue the inference; that is, continue if

$P(\text{MAX}) > M_L$ and
$P(\text{MIN}) < M_U$.

7.3.3   Discussion

The Bayesian approach is an attractive way of handling uncertainty. Nevertheless, one must be careful not use highly correlated evidence, because applying additional correlated evidence may result in meaningless changes in probabilities.

7.4   THE CERTAINTY-FACTOR APPROACH

The certainty factor (CF) was introduced in MYCIN, an early ES developed for medical diagnosis. A variation on probability theory, CF is composed of a measure of belief (MB) and a measure of disbelief (MD).

MB is a measure of a user's increased belief in hypothesis H, based on evidence E; MD is a measure of the user's increased disbelief in hypothesis H, based on the same evidence. Formally, MB and MD are defined as

$MB(H,E) = 1$ \qquad\qquad if $P(H) = 1$

$$= \frac{\max[P(H \mid E), P(H)] - P(H)}{1 - P(H)} \quad \text{if } 0 \leq P(H) < 1 \qquad (7.12)$$

and

$$MD(H,E)= 0 \qquad\qquad \text{if } P(H) = 0$$

$$= \frac{P(H) - \min[P(H \mid E), P(H)]}{P(H)} \quad \text{if } 0 < P(H) < 1 \qquad (7.13)$$

Using the above definitions, CF is defined as

$$CF(H,E) = MB(H,E) - MD(H,E). \qquad\qquad (7.14)$$

Some important properties of these measures are as follows:

i. $0 \le MB \le 1$

ii. $0 \le MD \le 1$

iii. $-1 \le CF \le 1$

Although CF ranges between -1 and 1, the basic concept is similar to that of the Bayesian approach.

Example 7.3

From Example 7.1, CF can be computed as follows:

MB (High, Electronics) $= (0.8 - 0.45) / (1 - 0.45) = .6364$
MD (High, Electronics) $= (0.45 - 0.45) / (0.45) = 0$
CF (High, Electronics) $= 0.6364$

The scheme used to compute a composite security grade in K-FOLIO is a variation on CF (see Section 6.4.2).

7.5   THE FUZZY-LOGIC APPROACH

7.5.1   Possibility Theory

The notion of *possibility* was proposed by Zadeh (1985) as an alternative to *probability*. Since possibility measures the degree of each event's occurrence on a [0,1] scale, it is easily understood by most decision makers. Suppose there is a stock whose possibility of achieving each of the grades is as follows:

Grade	A	B	C	D
Possibility	1	0.8	0.3	0

Note that the sum of the possibilities is not equal to 1. When uncertainty is represented by possibility, fuzzy logic can be applied.

7.5.2   Fuzzy Logic

Stock x's possibility of earning a high yield can be denoted as $P_S(\text{High}(x))$. The function $P_S(\cdot)$ is called a membership function, where

$$0 \le P_S(\cdot) \le 1.$$

Suppose $P_S(\text{High}(\text{Electronics})) = 0.8$. To integrate fuzzy evidence, the following basic AND, OR, and NOT operators are used:

$$P_1(\cdot) \text{ AND } P_2(\cdot) = \text{MIN } (P_1(\cdot), P_2(\cdot))$$
$$P_1(\cdot) \text{ OR } P_2(\cdot) = \text{MAX } (P_1(\cdot), P_2(\cdot))$$
$$\text{NOT } P_1(\cdot) = 1 - P_1(\cdot).$$

7.5.3   Fuzzy-Logic-based Expert System

The fuzzy-logic approach can be applied to an expert system. Suppose there are two rules with fuzziness as follows:

Example 7.4

    Rule 1
IF	<X> exports well	(1.0)
AND	<X> belongs to electronics industry	(0.6)
THEN	<X> provides high yield	

    Rule 2
IF	<X> belongs to a large conglomerate	(0.5)
AND	<X> has high R&D activity	(0.25)
THEN	<X> provides high yield	

where the variable <X> stands for the names of companies.

Any stock that satisfies rules 1 and/or 2 can be concluded to provide high yield with a given possibility. Since each rule has evidence in the AND relationship,

    Rule 1:   MIN(1.0, 0.6) = 0.6;
    Rule 2:   MIN(0.5, 0.25) = 0.25.

The two rules are next integrated by the OR relationship:

    Rule 1 or 2:   MAX(0.6, 0.25) = 0.6.

According to the system of fuzzy logic, it may be concluded that a stock <X> that satisfies either rule 1 or 2 provides high yield with the possibility 0.6.

7.5.4   A Compensatory Fuzzy-Logic Approach

One limitation of the pure fuzzy-logic approach is that much information can be lost during the evidence integration process. In Example 7.4, the information

<X>	exports well	(1.0)
<X>	belongs to a large conglomerate	(0.5)

was not used at all. To compensate for this deficiency, the following updating formula (Shortliffe 1976) may be used:

$$P_S (H: Rule\ i, Rule\ j)$$
$$= P_S (H: Rule\ i) + P_S (H: Rule\ j) (1 - P_S (H: Rule\ i)). \qquad (7.15)$$

Shortliffe originally called formula (7.15) the "measure of belief." But since his terminology may be confused with *MB* as defined in (7.12), it is best to refer to (7.15) as *Compensatory Fuzzy Logic*.

Example 7.5

For Example 7.4, (7.15) is applied:

$$P_S (High: Rule\ 1, Rule\ 2)$$
$$= P_S (High: Rule\ 1) + P_S(High: Rule\ 2) (1 - P_S(High: Rule\ 1))$$
$$= 0.6 + 0.25 (1 - 0.6)$$
$$= 0.75.$$

The concluded possibility of 0.75 differs from the value of 0.6 obtained by the non-compensatory fuzzy-logic approach. Although we cannot be sure which value is correct, the result obtained by using compensatory fuzzy logic seems more reasonable.

7.5.5   Attenuation by the Credibility of Rules

Thus far, it has been assumed that rules themselves are not uncertain, only the facts. In practice, this may not be the case. In order to attenuate the possibility of conclusion due to uncertainties in rules, the notion of the *credibility* of Rule *i*, or CR_i, may be introduced. In this case,

$$P_S \ (H: Rule \ i, \ Rule \ j)$$
$$= CR_i \ P_S \ (H: Rule \ i) + CR_j \ P_S \ (H: Rule \ j) \ (1 - P_S \ (H: Rule \ i)). \qquad (7.16)$$

Example 7.6

In Example 7.4, suppose

> *CR* of Rule 1 = 0.9
> *CR* of Rule 2 = 0.8.

The possibility that <X> provides high yield can be computed as

$$P_S(High: Rule \ 1, \ Rule \ 2)$$
$$= CR_1 \ P_S(High: Rule \ 1)$$
$$+ CR_2 \ P_S(High: Rule \ 2) \ (1 - P_S \ (High: Rule \ 1)) \qquad (7.17)$$
$$= (0.9) \ (0.6) + (0.8) \ (0.25) \ (1 - 0.6)$$
$$= 0.62.$$

Note that the possibility of obtaining a high yield has decreased from 0.75 to 0.62 because of attenuation.

7.5.6   Discussion

The fuzzy-logic approach has the advantages of representational compatibility with rules and a small computational burden. Nevertheless, in order to measure uncertainty about rules and facts, fuzzy logic requires as much data as the Bayesian approach.

7.6   NONMONOTONIC REASONING

One important feature of investment decisions is *nonmonotonic reasoning,* in which the accumulation of additional knowledge does not necessarily increase the number of derived facts (also called theorems). This phenomenon occurs when certain facts are implicitly assumed. If a newly acquired fact disproves previous assumptions, the facts derived from these assumptions should be modified. This process is called truth maintenance (Doyle 1979).

In securities investment, there are many things to be assumed. For example, some investors might have assumed the 1991 Persian Gulf Crisis would continue longer than six months. In this case the rules pertaining to that assumption should have been invoked and the rules of the contrary assumption, suppressed. Other implicit assumptions might relate to the political stability of former Soviet dominated nations, the progress of government regulations, the outcome of domestic elections, and so forth.

To invoke rules relevant to investor assumptions, one might begin with dialogue about assumptions for controversial issues. Then the system would invoke only those rules that are congruent with these assumptions.

7.7   CONCLUSIONS

Uncertainty handling methods include the Bayesian, certainty-factor, fuzzy-logic, and nonmonotonic reasoning approaches, which help decision makers to represent uncertain information and to render approximate reasoning. In the K-FOLIO system, a variant of the certainty factor approach and assumption-based reasoning (to overcome nonmonotonicity problems) are used. To fill the gap between the knowledge-providing expert's view and the system user's view, a sensitivity analysis capability is also provided.

REFERENCES

Doyle, J., 1979. A Truth Maintenance System. *Artificial Intelligence* 12: 231–72.

Kanal, L. N., and Lemmer, J. F., eds., 1986. *Uncertainty in Artificial Intelligence.* North-Holland.

Naylor, C., 1984. How to Build an Inferencing Engine. *In Expert Systems: Principles and Case Studies,* ed. Ru. Forsyth, Chapman and Hall Computing.

Shortliffe, E., 1976. *Computer-Based Medical Consultations: MYCIN.* New York: Elsevier Publishing Co.

Zadeh, C. V., 1985. *Expert Systems and Fuzzy Systems.* New York: Benjamin/Cummings Publishing Company, Inc.

CHAPTER 8

Knowledge Acquisition, Integration, and Maintenance

8.1   INTRODUCTION

In Chapters 5, 6, and 7, it was shown how knowledge relevant to investment decisions can be represented and how stocks and other securities can be inferentially evaluated by using knowledge. Questions still remain concerning where to acquire the required knowledge, how to design an efficient knowledge entry and maintenance process, and how to integrate multiple relevant knowledge bases (Gaines and Boose 1988). Hence, this chapter will discuss the representation of investor preferences and their integration with expert knowledge, sources for knowledge acquisition (human experts and machine-learning systems), the use of knowledge structuring and meta-knowledge to aid in the knowledge entry and maintenance process, and the selective integration of relevant knowledge in a way that does not compromise inference efficiency.

8.2   THE REPRESENTATION AND INTEGRATION OF INVESTOR PREFERENCES

Investors who make investment decisions generally rely not only on experts' knowledge, but also on their own knowledge, constraints, and preferences. Thus, it is necessary to develop a representation for these factors, referred to collectively as *preference,* and a methodology for timing and integrating preference with experts' knowledge.

8.2.1   The Organization of Investor Preference Bases

Two factors to be considered in representing investor preference are syntactic compatibility with experts' knowledge and the unique features of personal preference. Commonly shared expert knowledge may be used to evaluate stocks, but the decision of how much to invest must be made by the investor according to the investment model he or she uses. Because of this, the investor preference base should be distinguished from the expert knowledge base (see Figure 5.6). In the K-FOLIO system the expert knowledge base and investor preference bases are organized as shown in Figure 8.1 (Lee, Chu, and Kim 1989). Theoretically, every investor will have a unique preference base.

Figure 8.1
Organization of Expert Knowledge Bases and Investor Preference Bases

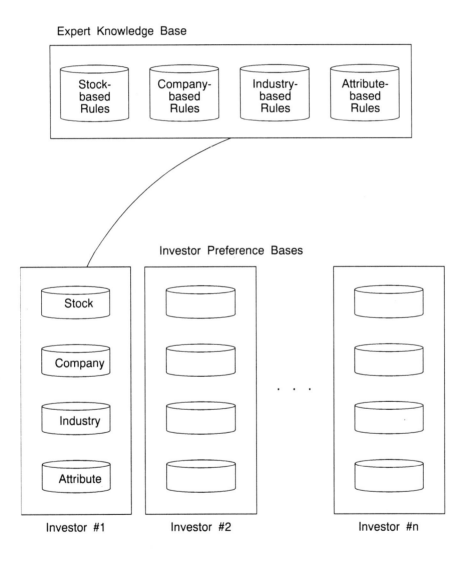

8.2.2   The Representation of Investor Preferences

The syntax of rules for expert knowledge representation was shown in Figure 6.2. Investor preference may be represented using a similar syntax, but if information about investment amounts is to be included, additional facilities will be needed. In K-FOLIO, the two reserved words AMOUNT and PERCENTAGE can be supported in the THEN part of the rules, as in the following examples:

Example 8.1

        RULE   rule 81
        CR = 0.7
        IF   Stock = C_1
        OR   Stock = C_2
        THEN   GRADE = AA
                AMOUNT ≤ 100,000
        AND   PERCENTAGE = 10%

According to Rule 81, the amount invested in stocks C_1 and/or C_2 should not exceed \$100,000, and the two stocks represent 10 percent of the portfolio.

Example 8.2

        RULE   rule 82
        CR = 0.8
        IF   Industry = I1
        THEN   AMOUNT ≤ 500,000
        OR   PERCENTAGE ≤ 20%
                EXCEPT C_3, C_4

Rule 82 limits the amount and percentage of total investment in industry I1 (excluding stocks C_3 and C_4).

Example 8.3

    RULE   rule 83

    CR = 0.9

    IF   P/E Ratio ≤ 7

    AND   Annual Sales Growth Rate ≥ 30%

    THEN   AMOUNT = 400,000

Rule 83 indicates that the investor wishes to invest $400,000 in stocks whose price-earning ratios are less than 7 and whose annual sales growth rates are greater than or equal to 30 percent.

8.2.3   The Integration and Interpretation of Preferences

Integration of the preferences of a specific investor (e.g., investor 1 in Figure 8.1) with expert knowledge can be achieved simply by merging corresponding rules (see Figure 8.2). Note, however, that this merge should occur only during the conflict-set generation process (Section 6.4). The original knowledge base and preference base should be kept intact.

Figure 8.2
Integrating Expert Knowledge and Investor Preference

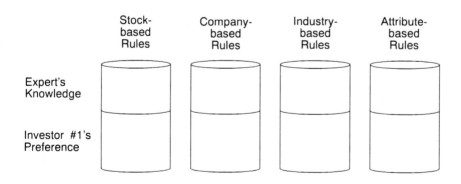

To resolve potential conflicts in grades and credibilities between expert knowledge and investor preferences, priority may be declared at global or rule level. For global declaration, either the statement

PRIORITY   =   EXPERT

or

PRIORITY   =   INVESTOR

may be used. To declare priority of preference at the rule level, the PRIORITY statement may appear within a rule, as in

RULE   rule 10
PRIORITY = OVERRIDE
CR = 0.8
IF   Company = XYX
THEN   GRADE = A
              BECAUSE . . .

OVERRIDE implies that the preference in Rule 10 takes precedence over any potentially conflicting expert knowledge. A YIELD statement implies the opposite.

In computing the composite grade encompassing expert knowledge and investor preferences, the grades in individual rules in the preference base may be treated in the same way as the ones in the expert knowledge base (see Section 6.2).

Preferences could be revealed during interactive dialogue with the screen, (see Figure 6.11). The user of the system may add new reasons, delete existing ones, and change grades and credibilities, but these modifications should not be stored in the preference base permanently. (The process of modification is illustrated in Figures 12.6 through 12.8.) Restrictions given by AMOUNT and PERCENTAGE in Examples 8.1 through 8.3 will be transformed into constraints in the optimization model for portfolio decisions described in Chapter 10.

8.3   SOURCES FOR KNOWLEDGE ACQUISITION

It is not difficult to find experts in various aspects of investing from whom to acquire knowledge, but there are few who regularly provide reliable knowledge for public use. One reason for this is that the computational complexity associated with making investment decisions is such that local heuristics are rarely consistent; thus, human experts' knowledge is generally ad hoc, biased, and localized. Automatic knowledge acquisition from a machine-learning system may be utilized to overcome such human expert limitations. Machine learning, to be discussed in the next chapter, may be used to automate the production of value-based investment rules from inputs such as financial ratios, and to produce synergistic sets of short-term trading rules that exploit recurrent short-persistence price anomalies.

Human experts are the only media from which one can collect nonrecurrent knowledge; thus, human-expert knowledge will always supplement machine-learned knowledge. K-FOLIO employs a mixed-knowledge acquisition strategy (see Figure 8.3).

Figure 8.3
Mixed-Knowledge Acquisition Strategy

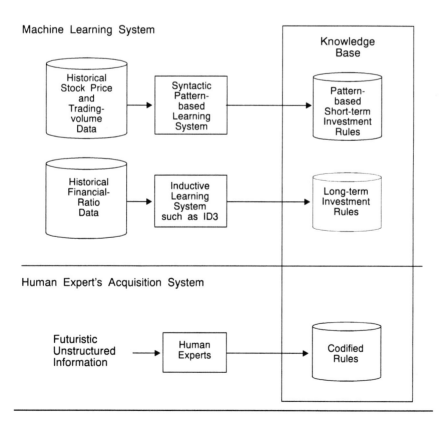

8.4   KNOWLEDGE STRUCTURE AND MAINTENANCE

8.4.1   Structuring Knowledge

In order to visualize the classification of rules, the subjects of rules can be abstracted in a hierarchical structure (see Figure 8.4). Subjects may be regarded as attributes in rules; a rule that includes more than one subject would be indexed by more than one parent subject. This classification structure is helpful for confirming and modifying the rules for a certain subject. Using frames, the hierarchical structure can be succinctly represented as follows:

{{Stock Evaluation
            FACTORS   : Financial Structure, Popularity}}

{{Financial Structure
            FACTORS   : Profitability, Growth}}

{{Popularity
            FACTORS   : Public Preference, Leading Stock}}

{{Profitability
            RULES   : rule 30, rule 41, rule 52, rule 73}}

{{Growth
            RULES   : rule 35, rule 43, rule 55}}

{{Public Preference
            RULES   : rule 12, rule 38}}

{{Leading Stock
            RULES   : rule 27, rule 49, rule 78}}

When a rule is inputted or changed, the subject structure should be displayed so as to cue the user to enter or possibly revise the classifica-

Figure 8.4
Hierarchical Knowledge Structuring by Subject

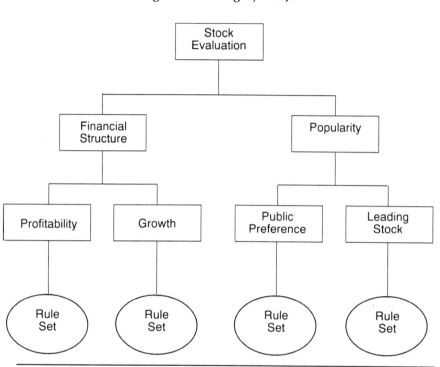

tion. In order to maintain consistency between the rule set and subject indices, the system may conservatively reject the storage of a new rule unless the associated subject is confirmed.

8.4.2   Maintenance Aids

Meta-knowledge (knowledge about knowledge) is useful for maintaining knowledge. Relevant meta-knowledge includes the usage of knowledge (whether for evaluation of individual stocks or for general equity buy/sell timing decisions), investment horizon (long; medium; or short-term), author, entry date, and expiration date. Meta-knowledge may be represented by extending the rule syntax in Figure 6.2 to the format shown in Figure 8.5.

Figure 8.5
Extended Syntax of Rules That Include Meta-Knowledge

```
{{RULE      rulename
     CREDIBILITY: percentage
     IF :     statement A
       (AND  statement B)
       (OR    statement C)
       . . .
     THEN : [statement ZZ
              GRADE = grade]
              (BECAUSE  statement)
              (EXCEPT statement)
     USAGE : [evaluation  buy/sell]
     HORIZON : [long   medium  short]
     AUTHOR : name
     ENTRY-DATE : date
     EXPIRATION-DATE : date }}
```

Legend

> Capital letter : reserved words
> ( ) : optional statement
> [ ] : one of the statements should be chosen

Using meta-knowledge, knowledge engineers can retrieve rules that satisfy criteria, such as the following:

1. What knowledge did George enter during October 1991?

2. What knowledge expires today?

3. What knowledge is available for evaluating stocks from a long-term investment perspective?

Through the meta-knowledge facility, inquiries about all possible combinations of USAGE, HORIZON, AUTHOR, ENTRY-DATE, and EXPI-

RATION-DATE can be retrieved; this will improve knowledge maintenance productivity.

8.5   THE SELECTIVE INTEGRATION OF RELEVANT
KNOWLEDGE

Knowledge critical for short-term investment decisions may be relatively
unimportant for long-term investment, and vice versa. For example,
short-duration excess returns may have little effect on long-holding-pe-
riod returns; therefore, it is desirable to classify the usage of knowledge
(see Section 8.4.2).

Another factor to be considered is the user's set of assumptions
about the environment. Different people would probably give different
answers to questions such as, *Will the current international crisis last
more than a month? Will the economy recover this year? Will the U.S.
dollar be stronger or weaker over the next 18 months?* Depending on
the answer to a particular question, or assumption, the relevant portion
of the knowledge base will vary; thus, knowledge must be linked with
assumptions. Syntactically speaking, the assumption may be regarded as
another type of attribute; nevertheless, differentiating assumptions from
other attributes is helpful in dialogue. For example, consider the two
following assumptions about a hypothetical Mideast Crisis, long- or
short-lasting:

{{ASSUMPTION: Mideast Crisis lasts long
   THEN: Oil price hikes}}
{{RULE   automobile
   IF: Oil price hikes
   AND: Industry = automobile
   THEN: Grade = C}}

{{ASSUMPTION: Mideast Crisis lasts short
   THEN: Oil price declines}}

{{RULE   automobile
   IF: Oil price declines
   AND: Industry = automobile
   THEN: Grade = A}}

If the user assumes that the Mideast Crisis will last long, then there will be an unfavorable grade for the automobile industry; if the user assumes the opposite, the automobile industry will receive a favorable grade. Therefore, environmental assumptions should be elicited at the beginning of dialogue so that the system can select only the relevant knowledge bases. Some common assumptions would be those associated with strength of the dollar, continuation of expansion or recession, labor relations climate, inflation outlook, and political outcomes. Figure 12.2 shows the typical dialogue associated with various environmental assumptions.

8.6   CONCLUSIONS

Knowledge acquisition is crucial to any expert system, and it becomes a serious problem if human experts cannot effectively provide knowledge. One solution is the use of machine learning, to be discussed in the next chapter. A system generally has multiple knowledge bases developed from several acquisitional sources (human experts, investor, and machine learning); therefore, it is inevitable that, depending on its source, knowledge will be selectively integrated into the system in various ways. As knowledge maintenance under these conditions is very complex and error-prone, the hierarchical structuring of knowledge and the use of meta-knowledge are useful methods to follow.

REFERENCES

Lee, J. K., Chu, S., and Kim, H., 1989. *Intelligent Stock Portfolio Management System.* Expert Systems 6 (April): 74–87.

Gaines, B. R., and Boose, J. H., eds, 1988. *Knowledge Acquisition for Knowledge-based Systems,* Vols. 1 and 2: Academic Press.

CHAPTER 9

Machine Learning and Neural Networks

9.1   INTRODUCTION

9.1.1   Why Machine Learning?

Machine learning is a medium for automatic knowledge acquisition that can be used when expert knowledge (1) does not exist, (2) is not sufficiently reliable, (3) is prohibitively expensive, or (4) is not available in a continuous and timely manner. Unfortunately, knowledge in the investment domain is characterized by all of these features to varying degrees. In the experience of the authors, as well as that of others that have built ES for this domain, it is extremely difficult to find human investment consultants who are competent, cooperative, and reliable enough to consistently provide superior knowledge for formal public use. Thus, it appears that automatic knowledge acquisition through machine learning is an essential element of expert systems for investment management.

9.1.2   Machine-Learning Systems

Auto-learning systems were briefly described in Chapter 4. *Machine learning* refers to specific mechanisms through which learning may take place in an auto-learning system (see Figure 9.1). The system generates knowledge, from both the environment and critics, concerning the gap between real-world results and the expert system's output. The goal is to transform environmental and critics' responses into the form of knowledge discussed in Section 6.2. One difficulty in learning from critics is that any gap that exists could be the result of both deficiencies in the quality of knowledge generated from machine learning and the adequacy of inference. Nevertheless, if the inference scheme is frozen, fluctuations in the quality of the system's output can be attributed solely to the effectiveness of the machine-learning scheme.

9.1.3   Learning Strategies

Learning strategies that have received significant attention in AI literature include inductive learning, syntactic-pattern-based learning, genetic adaptive algorithms, neural networks, case-based learning and reasoning, and learning by taking advice. This chapter will review concepts common to all learning strategies, then evaluate the potential of several ap-

Figure 9.1
Machine-Learning Procedure

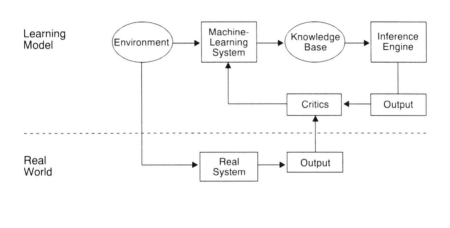

proaches and show how these can be used for investment knowledge generation. At present, it appears that the most popular and promising approaches for investment decisions are those of inductive, neural network, and syntactic-pattern-based learning, so these three will be given special attention.

9.2   IMPLIED DISTRIBUTION SURROGATES

As discussed in Section 2.6.2, historical security-price and trading-volume series contain valuable, though incomplete, information about share-acquisition-cost distributions. To the extent that the price paid for a security will influence subsequent liquidation-price and timing decisions, the security's market supply ought to be impacted by the cost-distribution parameters. There is evidence that it is not necessary to have a lengthy history of trading data in order to generate effective rules based on this concept. As will be seen, statistically significant qualitative predictions of short-term price movements have been achieved by using collections of rules derived over relatively short time frames. The reason for this is probably that a substantial portion of the activity on most issues is attributable to regular traders, including specialists, who continually revise their holdings of the security.

Combinations of primitives (features) from two or more time-series charts of price, volume, moving averages, correlations, and so on may be utilized as surrogates for implied price distributions, which (for reasons discussed in Section 2.6.2) cannot be represented quantitatively with any degree of precision. Consider, for example, the following combinations and probable (but not certain) implications for the distribution of share costs over a given time frame:

Price random, high volatility $\Rightarrow$ wide uniform distribution

Price random, low volatility $\Rightarrow$ narrow uniform distribution

Price trend up, volume constant $\Rightarrow$ uniform distribution,
mean below current price

Price trend up, volume decreasing $\Rightarrow$ trapezoidal distribution,
mean below current price

Price trend up, volume low - then high - then low $\Rightarrow$ unimodal
distribution, mean below current price

Price trend down, volume high - then low - then high $\Rightarrow$ bimodal
distribution, mean above current price

Price up - then down, volume constant $\Rightarrow$ uniform distribution,
mean above current price

Relationships such as those above can be converted to rules by using Bayesian, certainty-factor, or fuzzy-logic approaches (see Chapter 7). Since the exact mechanisms through which distribution characteristics impact supply demand equilibrium are unknown and probably dynamic, one may skip directly to price-change predictions as the conclusions of such rules. Employment of chart primitives in such a surrogate role is not to be confused with naive conventional chartist methodologies. The advantages of using chart primitives for representation are that they can be rapidly extracted from existing raw data; they do not suffer from ambiguity; and when graphically displayed they can aid in the explanation process.

9.3   INDUCTIVE LEARNING

Software tools for inductive learning are widely available. Inductive learning is also called learning-from-example. Popular products such as EXPERT-EASE and VP-EXPERT are equipped with such a learning facility.

9.3.1   ID3

ID3 was one of the first inductive-learning algorithms. According to Quinlan (1979), ID3 generates rules by the procedure shown in Figure 9.2. First one selects *instances* (i.e., cases, occurrences, or historical examples), which constitute a set called the *window*. The window, in conjunction with the *concept-learning algorithm*, is used to generate rules (see Section 9.3.2). If the rule can cover the entire set of instances, the rule set is perfect; otherwise, exceptional instances are incrementally included into the window to improve the current rule set. This procedure is continued until the formed rule set becomes perfect or at least meets some minimum criterion of satisfaction.

9.3.2   The Concept-Learning Algorithm

The concept-learning algorithm constructs decision trees by using a top-down, divide-and-conquer approach (Michalski et al 1983). Assume that there are two graphs, referred to as Charts 1 and 2, from which for each instance, two kinds of attributes and a scalar measure can be drawn. These graphs can be combined with a price-change conclusion column (see Figure 9.3). The attributes of Charts 1 and 2 are varying patterns, while numeric percentages are represented in the column Numeric 3. The observed price change for each instance is classified into one of three classes: *up, down,* or *sustained.* From these instances, the concept-learning algorithm first selects the attribute that has the highest discriminating power with respect to price change. In this example, Chart 1 has the highest discriminating power, so it is placed at the top of the classifying tree. The occurrence of pattern 1B in Chart 1 provides sufficient

Figure 9.2
ID3 Algorithm

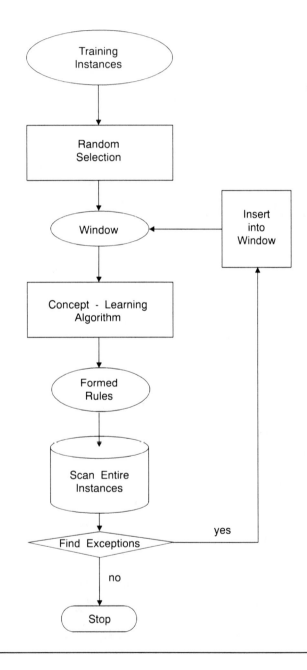

Figure 9.3
Inductive-Learning Procedure

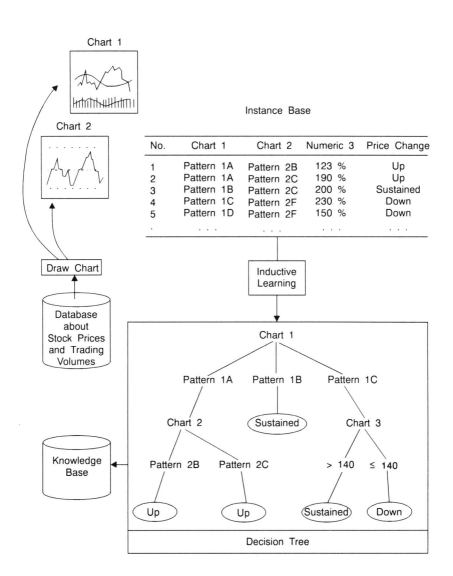

Chart 1

Chart 2

Instance Base

No.	Chart 1	Chart 2	Numeric 3	Price Change
1	Pattern 1A	Pattern 2B	123 %	Up
2	Pattern 1A	Pattern 2C	190 %	Up
3	Pattern 1B	Pattern 2C	200 %	Sustained
4	Pattern 1C	Pattern 2F	230 %	Down
5	Pattern 1D	Pattern 2F	150 %	Down
.	. . .	. . .	. . .	. . .

Draw Chart

Inductive Learning

Database about Stock Prices and Trading Volumes

Chart 1

Pattern 1A   Pattern 1B   Pattern 1C

Chart 2   Sustained   Chart 3

Knowledge Base

Pattern 2B   Pattern 2C   > 140   ≤ 140

Up   Up   Sustained   Down

Decision Tree

evidence to conclude that the price change is "sustained"; pattern 1A, however, needs additional information from Chart 2 to reach a conclusion, and pattern 1C needs information from Numeric 3 to reach a conclusion. This process continues until there are no ambiguous conclusions left. To measure discriminating power, Quinlan uses the following *entropy* metric:

$$\text{Entropy} = \sum_{i=1}^{k} [-\frac{n_i}{\sum_i n_i} \log_k (n_i / \sum_i n_i)]$$

(9.1)

where k is the number of classes and n_i is the number of instances in the conclusion class i.

For example, if the numbers of patterns in Chart 1 for the three classes are $n_{up} = 0$, $n_{down} = 0$, and $n_{sustained} = 30$, the entropy for Chart 1 becomes zero, because Chart 1 can classify these instances without any ambiguity. Another extreme example is $n_{up} = 10$, $n_{down} = 10$, and $n_{sustained} = 10$, in which case Chart 1 does not have any discriminating power at all, so its entropy is 1. When $n_{up} = 20$, $n_{down} = 10$, and $n_{sustained} = 0$, the entropy value is 0.579. Thus the degree of conformity among the instances in a class can provide a reasonable measure of credibility for rules (see Section 6.2).

A decision tree generated by the concept-learning algorithm can be transformed into rules. The decision tree in Figure 9.3, for example, implies the following rules:

IF	*Chart 1 = Pattern 1A*
AND	*Chart 2 = Pattern 2B*
THEN	*Price Change = Up*

IF	*Chart 1 = Pattern 1A*
AND	*Chart 2 = Pattern 2C*
THEN	*Price Change = Up*

IF	*Chart 1 = Pattern 1B*
THEN	*Price Change = Sustained*

IF   Chart 1 = Pattern 1C

AND   Numeric 3 > 140%

THEN   Price Change = Sustained

IF   Chart 1 = Pattern 1C

AND   Numeric 3 ≤ 140%

THEN   Price Change = Down

9.3.3   Application of Inductive Learning to Investment Decisions

In their 1987 study, Braun and Chandler adopted the ID3 approach in an attempt to predict stock market movements (see Chapter 4). the authors used 20 attributes out of the potential cues listed in Table 9.1, which generated a set of rules from 108 examples collected weekly at the Friday close of market; these rules predicted correctly 64.4 percent of the time. The three classes employed were bullish (predicting an upward trend), bearish (predicting a downward trend), and neutral (predicting a sideways market). These classifications were prepared in order to provide moderate-risk and aggressive investors with weekly recommendations. Since a single investment analyst had selected and interpreted the attributes and outcomes for the preparation of the experimental data, the rule set undoubtedly reflected the biases of this particular expert.

In an experiment by Kim et al, (1987, 1988) in pattern-based inductive learning, the success ratio on two classes of movement (up or down) ranged from 68 percent to 74.15 percent. This study employed 7 attributes: 25-, 75-, and 150-day moving averages of stock prices, 6- and 25-day moving averages of trading volumes, a price-trading volume correlation curve, a volume ratio, and a psychological line. The rules used for performance evaluation in Chapter 10 were also generated by the concept-learning algorithm. In this case, 18 attributes were used to classify stocks into 5 classes.

9.3.4   The Potential of Inductive Learning in Investment

The inductive-learning technique can be used to generate rules that classify stocks and bonds into grades. In using the technique for fundamen-

---

Table 9.1
Potential Cues

1. Put-call ratio, Chicago Board of Options Exchange (PCCBOE)[a]
2. Put-call ratio, American Options Exchange (PCAMEX)[a]
3. Granville Cumulative Climax Indicator (GCCI), nonconfirmation cumulative climax[c]
4. GCCI, retrogress (GRANRET)[a]
5. GCCI, trend (GRANTRN)[a]
6. Weinstein Last-Hour Activity, volume NYSE index nonconfirmation[c]
7. Weinstein Last-Hour Activity, volume NYSE index trend[c]
8. Weinstein Last-Hour Activity, price DJI nonconfirmation[c]
9. Weinstein Last-Hour Activity, price DJI trend[c]
10. Dow Jones moving average, 10-day cycle (DJI10)[a]
11. Dow Jones moving average, 30-day cycle (DJI30)[a]
12. Dow Jones moving average, conjointly (when DJI10 = DJI30)[b]
13. On-balance volume DJI, trend (OBVDOW)[a]
14. On-balance volume DJI, nonconfirmation
15. Cash of DJI, trend (CASHDOW)[a]
16. Cash of DJI, nonconfirmation (NETCDOW)[a]
17. Specialist short sales, ratio vs. odd-lot sales (SSOLS)[a]
18. Specialist short sales, 4-week moving vs. total shorts (SSTS)[a]
19. Market pressure index, 1-day moving average (MPI)[a]
20. Omtemsotu DJI, trend (expert's trend model)[b]
21. Intensity DJI, nonconfirmation (expert's trend model)[b]
22. Dow theory, compare transportation to industrials[b]
23. Dow theory, over-bought over-sold oscillator (OBOSOS)[a]

---

[a]Variable used as cue to develop rule
[b]Variable primarily for long-term fluctuations
[c]Unable to use because of insufficient data
Source: Braun and Chandler, 1987

Table 9.1 *(continued)*

24. NYSE composite index, trend and field trend (NYSECI)[a]
25. NYSE composite index, nonconfirmation vs. DJI price index[c]
26. Dow Jones Industrial, trend and field trend (DJIFT)[a]
27. Dow Jones Transportation, trends and field trend (DJTT)[a]
28. Dow Jones Transportation, trend breaks (DJTTB)[a]
29. S&P front spread, trend[c]
30. S&P front spread, nonconfirmation[c]
31. Cash of DJI Weekly, trend[b]
32. Cash of DJI Weekly, nonconfirmation[b]
33. Dow Jones figure point objective, 5 points[c]
34. Dow Jones figure point objective, 10 points[c]
35. Optimism-pessimism index, trend[c]
36. Optimism-pessimism index, nonconfirmation[c]
37. Optimism-pessimism index, 10-point figure chart[c]
38. Optimism-pessimism index, 25-point figure chart[c]
39. Wycoff Wave, trend (WWTRN)[a]
40. Wycoff Wave, nonconfirmation (WWREV)[a]
41. Trend barometer, momentum[b]
42. Trend barometer, force[b]
43. Trend barometer, technometer[b]
44. Ratio of ratios, trend of 6-day ratio[b]
45. Ratio of ratios, value of 6-day ratio (RATRAT)[a]
46. Ratio of ratios, trend of 10-day ratio[b]
47. Ratio of ratios, value of 10-day ratio[b]

tal analysis, attributes should be selected from the financial data with the longest evaluation time lag. On the other hand, in using inductive learning for stock analysis based on trading data, patterns should be automatically detected from charts and evaluated by using a very short time lag (see Section 9.4). When used for classification problems, the inductive-learning scheme seems to compete well with the syntactic-pattern-based learning and neural network approaches to be discussed next.

9.4   SYNTACTIC-PATTERN-BASED LEARNING

In the syntactic-pattern-recognition approach, patterns are viewed as complexes of *primitives* and *compositional operators,* and the structure of legitimate patterns is analogous to the syntactic grammar of language. This approach has been applied to a variety of scientific domains, including the classification of fingerprints (Rao and Black 1980) and carotid pulse waves (Stockman et al. 1976). However, there has been little syntactic-pattern-recognition research oriented toward security investment applications. Kandt and Yuenger (1988) describe a system under development that appears to include a syntactic-pattern-recognition capability, but they offer no details about the mechanism or performance of the system. We will discuss next a price-pattern-recognition system, SYNPLE, that is based on syntactic-pattern-learning theory (Lee, Kim, and Trippi 1991).

9.4.1   SYNPLE Framework

SYNPLE is a system that recognizes primitives contained in charts, and synthesizes legitimate patterns with the highest probability of classification power. SYNPLE has four steps, as follows:

Selection of Charts

The first step of the syntactic-pattern-recognition approach is to select appropriate charts. In this example, the charts are stock-price trend lines (Figure 9.4), moving-average curves of stock price (Figure 9.5), moving-average curves of trading volume (Figure 9.6), and a price-volume correlation curve (Figure 9.7).

Figure 9.4
Illustrative Stock-Price Trend Lines

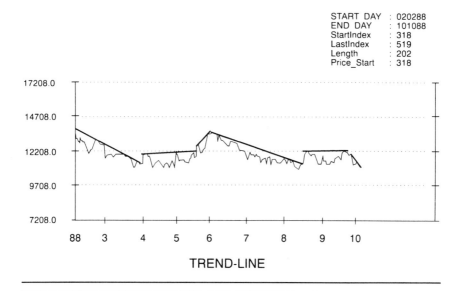

```
START DAY   : 020288
END DAY     : 101088
StartIndex  : 318
LastIndex   : 519
Length      : 202
Price_Start : 318
```

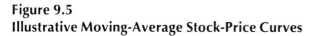

TREND-LINE

Figure 9.5
Illustrative Moving-Average Stock-Price Curves

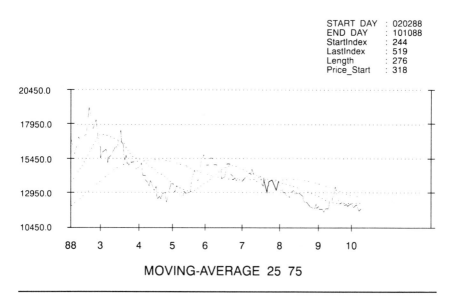

```
START DAY   : 020288
END DAY     : 101088
StartIndex  : 244
LastIndex   : 519
Length      : 276
Price_Start : 318
```

MOVING-AVERAGE 25 75

Figure 9.6
Illustrative Moving-Average Trading-Volume Curves

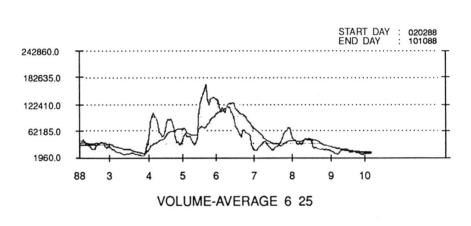

VOLUME-AVERAGE 6 25

Figure 9.7
Illustrative Price-Volume Correlation Curve

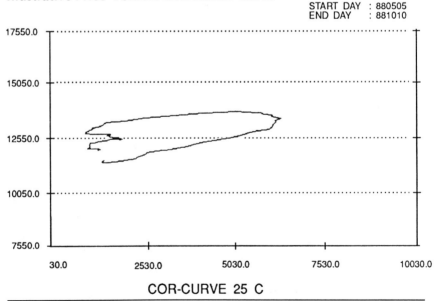

COR-CURVE 25 C

Definition of Elements

From each of the selected charts, users define those elements that they would like to detect. (An element is a *preprimitive* that lacks information about the duration of the occurrences.) Elements are specified by the composition of attributes and their corresponding values (see Table 9.2). For instance, an element from the trend-line type is

$\{\{TLP - 1$

　　$LINE\text{-}TYPE : central\text{-}line$

　　$TOLERANCE : 20$

　　$SLOPE : 0 \quad 20$

　　$SHIFT\text{-}AT\text{-}TAIL : up\}\}.$　　　　　　　　　　　　　　　(9.2)

The element *TLP-1* means that the line type is the central line of stock price with a tolerance of average error of 20. (A smaller tolerance indicated a tighter fit to the local trend.) The slope of the line belongs to the interval of 0 to 20 degrees, and the beginning point of the succeeding line is shifted upward. One hundred and fifty-eight such elements have been defined by using the reserved attributes and values in Table 9.2.

Definition of Duration

Care must be taken in attaching duration to the elements defined above, because the primitive could lead to a different conclusion depending upon the length of its duration. This is apparent from an examination of the sensitivity to duration of the lower supporting line, with a tolerance of 10 and a slope interval of [45, 90] (see Figure 9.8).

   i.   If duration ≤ 6 days, the mean price moves upward.

   ii.   If $6 <$ duration ≤ 16, the mean price is sustained.

   iii. If duration > 16, the mean price moves downward.

The primitive is fully defined by attaching duration to the element.

Table 9.2
Illustrative Elements Specified by Charts, Attributes, and Values

Chart	Attribute	Values
Trend Line of Stock Price	• Line-type	central line, upper supporting line, lower supporting line
	• Tolerance	40, 60, 80 (central line) 10, 15, 20 (upper supporting line, lower supporting line)
	• Slope	(–90, 45), (–45, –20), (–20, 0), (0, 20), (20, 45), (45, 90)
	• Shift-Direction	Shift-Up, Shift-Down
	• Gap	Wider, Narrower (between upper supporting line and lower supporting line)
Moving Average of Stock Price	• Slope	increase, decrease
	• Rate-of-Slope-Change	increase, decrease
	• Length	1, 6, 25, 75
	• Gap	narrower, wider (between 1-day and 6-day, 6-day and 25-day, 1-day and 25-day, 25-day and 75-day moving averages)
	• Relative-Position	above, below (between 1-day and 6-day, 6-day and 25-day, 1-day and 25-day, 25-day and 75-day moving averages)
Moving Average of Trading Volume	• Slope	increase, decrease
	• Length	6, 25, 75
	• Gap	narrower, wider (between 1-day and 6-day, 6-day and 25-day, 1-day and 25-day, 25-day and 75-day moving averages)
	• Relative-Position	above, below (with 1-day and 6-day, 6-day and 25-day, 1-day and 25-day, 25-day and 75-day moving averages)
Price-Volume Correlation Curve	• MAP-Slope	increase, decrease, sustain
	• MAV-Slope	increase, decrease, sustain
	• Length	25, 75

Figure 9.8
Sensitivity of Duration in Lower Support Line to Stock-Price Trend Line

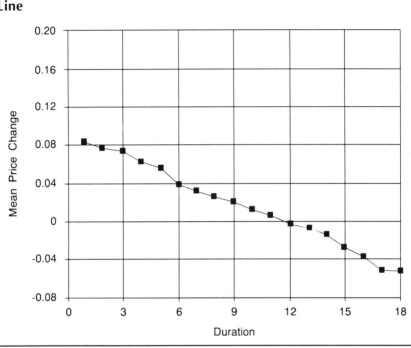

Synthesis of Patterns

The SYNPLE algorithm detects the primitives defined above, and selects the conclusion class with the highest probability of occurrence. This process builds primitive-based rules, each of which has a pattern (set of primitives) as a condition with a corresponding conclusion class. Probability in this context is essentially the same as the *credibility* of the rule. Primitives are composed into patterns via the operators *CONCURRENCE* and *SEQUENTIAL*; this process eventually leads to more complex patterns with higher credibility, and continues until a sufficient level of credibility is established or until no further improvement occurs.

9.4.2   Performance

In an empirical test of SYNPLE that used Korean stock-market data taken from the period from April 22, 1987 to October 22, 1987, the numbers of pattern instances detected and synthesized into the stock price "up" class was 1,857; the number detected and synthesized into the "down" class was 1,187. Three hundred ex ante rules were generated from the composed instances. As summarized in Table 9.3, the normalized mean actual stock price in the "up" class of 0.2398 is significantly higher than the –0.2015 of the "down" class. The rules generated from the first period data were tested on the four succeeding periods.

The mean next-period price of stocks in the "up" class is significantly higher than prices in the "down" class, with p-value being less than 0.0001 for all four subsequent test periods. The results are shown graphically in Figure 9.9. One peculiar feature is the performance of period 2's "down" class. In this period, even the average "down" class stock increased in value, most likely because of the 24th Olympic Games which were held in Seoul. Based on these preliminary results, the syntactic-pattern-based learning approach appears to be a promising one.

9.5   GENETIC ADAPTIVE ALGORITHMS

The genetic-adaptive-algorithm approach to learning was proposed by Holland (1975). Genetic algorithms are an effective approach to limiting search effort over large combinatorial search spaces. The essence of a genetic algorithm for machine learning is the systematic evaluation of the current generation of rules and the propagation of new rules (see Fig. 9.10). The algorithm starts with an initial rule set, which may be generated randomly. In each iteration, t, every rule R_i, is evaluated by a certain measure, such as the credibility of the rule. Rules with the lower scores on this measure, denoted $U(R_i(_t))$ in Figure 9.10, are discarded. New rules are generated by genetic operators that include crossover, mutation, and inversion. A genetic algorithm was used to generate the Poker Axiom, which was perfectly attained after 4,200 iterations.

Although there are not many situations in which the Holland operators can be applied directly to investment decisions, genetic algorithms can be applied indirectly through syntactic-pattern-based learning. New rules may be generated by systematically modifying values such as those in Table 9.2 with the use of a genetic algorithm to seek improvements.

Table 9.3
Performance of Generated Rules

		1st 4/22/87–10/22/87	2nd 10/23/87–4/22/88	3rd 4/23/88–10/22/88	4th 10/23/88–4/22/89	5th 4/22/89–10/22/89	Average (2–5th)
Overall mean		-0.0109	0.0803	0.0347	0.0811	-0.0695	
Class "Up"	mean	0.2398	0.2515	0.1837	0.1826	0.0942	0.188
	variance	0.01915	0.01708	0.01370	0.01187	0.00416	
	credibility	0.925	0.825	0.830	0.758	0.971	0.823
	instances	1,857	2,583	5,929	3,381	1,189	
Class "Down"	mean	-0.2015	0.0444	-0.1265	-0.1030	-0.0914	-0.093
	variance	0.00135	0.00106	0.00163	0.00053	0.00001	
	credibility	1.000	0.293	0.973	0.995	0.990	0.921
	instances	1,187	167	445	936	200	
z-value		130.37	57.41	126.76	141.42	98.83	
p-value		< 0.0001	< 0.0001	< 0.0001	< 0.0001	< 0.0001	

Figure 9.9
Mean Price Change by the Rules Generated From the First Data Set

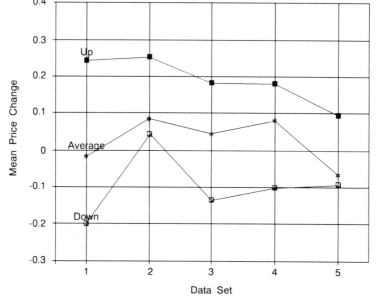

9.6   THE NEURAL-NETWORK APPROACH TO PRICE PREDICTION

As discussed in Chapter 4, neural networks can be used effectively in classifying and estimating nonlinear models with qualitative as well as quantitative inputs. This section will summarize three studies that specifically examine the effectiveness of neural networks for stock price movement prediction.

9.6.1   The Yoon and Swales Network

Yoon and Swales (1991) adopted a four-layered network (see Figure 9.11) with nine input parameters: confidence, economic factors outside the firm's control, growth, strategic plans, new products, anticipated loss, anticipated gain, long-term optimism, and short-term optimism. These factors were selected from studies of Fortune 500 and *Business Week's* Top 1000 firms. Output parameters have two nodes: well-per-

Figure 9.10
Genetic Adaptive Algorithm

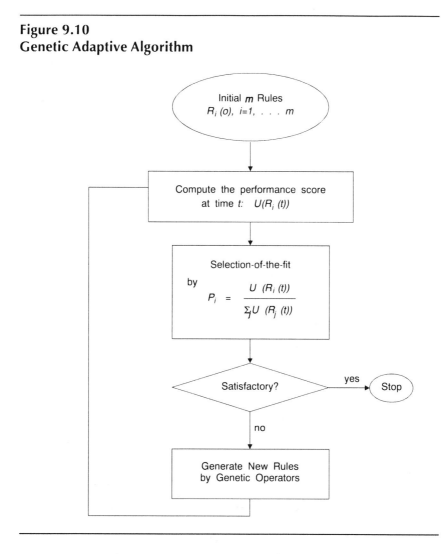

forming and poorly-performing firms. Fifty-eight cases were used for training, and the trained network was applied to 40 cases. Eighteen out of 20 (90%) well-performing firms were correctly classified, while 13 out of 20 (65%) poorly-performing firms were correctly classified. On the average, 77.5% of test cases were correctly classified. This result outperforms the classifying power of Multiple Discriminant Analysis, which correctly classified only 65%.

Figure 9.11
Four-Layered Network

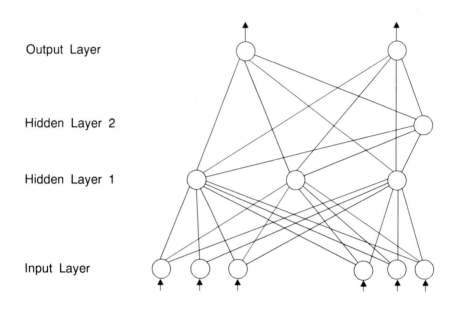

Output Layer

Hidden Layer 2

Hidden Layer 1

Input Layer

9.6.2   The NEC Network

Kamijo and Tanigawa (1990) developed a recurrent neural network model to predict a price pattern, called the "triangle" pattern, from a candlestick chart (see Figure 9.12). The candlestick is a symbol that shows opening, closing, high, and low prices for the week. For a white (black) candlestick, the opening (closing) price is lower than the closing (opening) price, and the top and bottom of the candlestick represent the closing (opening) and the opening (closing) prices. The vertical lines on the top and beneath the bottom that run through the candlestick depict high and low prices during the period. The two oblique lines in the triangle pattern are also called resistance lines, which to a traditional chartists implies the beginning of a sudden stock-price rise.

Figure 9.12
Candlestick Chart and Triangle Pattern

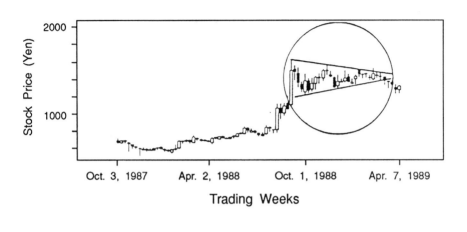

The normalized high, low, and average prices from this chart were input to the neural network, and the output was recurrently used as input for the next time period; the eventual output is the confirmation of the occurrence of triangles. After the network was trained for 15 triangle patterns by iterating 2,000 times, it correctly classified 15 out of 16 test cases.

9.6.3   The Fujitsu and Nikko Network

Kimoto, Asakawa, Yoda, and Takeoka (1990), under the sponsorship of Fujitsu Laboratories and Nikko securities, developed a network to determine optimal buy-and-sell timing for TOPIX (Tokyo Stock Exchange Price Index). The network's input parameters are vector curve, turnover, interest rate, foreign-exchange rate, Dow-Jones average, and several others. A single output node signals whether to buy or sell; an output value equal to or greater than 0.5 indicates "buy," while a value of less than 0.5 indicates "sell." The network was trained and tested by using monthly data from the period of January 1987 to September 1989. The performance of the network's buy-and-sell strategy is compared with

---

Figure 9.13
Performance of the Prediction System

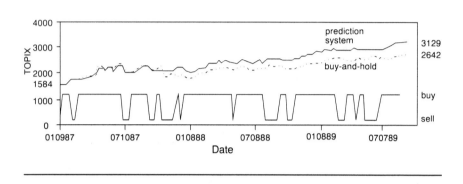

that of a buy-and-hold strategy (see Figure 9.13). The terminal investment value of 3,129 at September 1989, which would have resulted
from following the neural network model recommendations, exceeds the
2,642 TOPIX value at that date by 487 points—a significant difference.

9.7   CONCLUSIONS

Because of both the difficulty of acquiring superior knowledge from humans in a timely manner and the proprietary problems associated with
human-expert knowledge sources, adopting machine-learning mechanisms for rule generation is the key to success for systems to make
investment decisions. Machine learning is especially applicable to the
generation of synergistic sets of rules that exploit subtle or highly con-
volved price anomalies.

REFERENCES

Braun, H., and Chandler, J. S., 1987. Predicting Stock Market Behavior
Through Rule Induction: An Application of the Learning-from-Example
Approach. *Decision Sciences* 18: 415–29.

Holland, J. H., 1975. *Adaptation in Natural and Artificial Systems.* Ann
Arbor: University of Michigan Press.

Kamijo, K., and Tanigawa, T., 1990. Stock Price Pattern Recognition: A Recurrent Neural Network Approach. *Proceedings of the International Join Conference on Neural Networks,* San Diego, IEEE Neural Network Council, Vol. 1, 215–21.

Kandt, K., and Yuenger, P., 1988. A Financial Investment Assistant. *Proceedings of the 21st Annual Hawaii International Conference on Systems Sciences,* 510–17.

Kim, H. S., Chu, S. C., and Lee, J. K., 1988. Stock Investment Rule Generation by Inductive Learning: Korean Stock Market Case. KAIST Working Paper.

Kim, H. S., 1987. Generating Rules by Inductive Machine Learning: Exploratory Application to Stock Investment. Unpublished masters thesis. Seoul: Korea Advanced Institute of Science and Technology, Department of Management Science.

Kimoto, T., Asakawa, K., Yoda, M., and Takeoka, M., 1990. Stock Market Prediction System with Modular Neural Networks. *Proceedings of the International Joint Conference on Neural Networks,* San Diego, IEEE Network Council, Vol. 1, 1–6.

Lee, J. K., Kim, H. S., and Trippi, R. R., 1991. Syntactic Pattern-based Inductive Learning for Trading Rule Generation. KAIST Working Paper.

Michalski, R. S., Carbonell, J. G., and Michell, T. M., 1983. *Machine Learning: An Artificial Intelligence Approach.* Palo Alto: Tioga Publishing.

Quinlan, J. R., 1979. Discovering Rules by Induction from Large Collections of Examples. *Expert Systems in the Micro Electronic Age,* ed. D. Michie, Edinburgh: Edinburgh University Press.

Rao, K., and Black, K., 1980. Type Classification of Fingerprints: A Syntactic Approach. *IEEE Transactions of Pattern Analysis and Machine Intelligence* PAMI-2(3): 223–31.

Stockman, G., Kanal, L., and Kyle, M. C., 1976. Structural Pattern Recognition of Carotid Pulse Waves Using a General Waveform Parsing System. *Communications of the ACM* 19: 688–95.

Yoon, Y. and Swales, G., 1991. Predicting Stock Price Performance: A Neural Network Approach. *Proceedings of the 24th Annual Hawaii International Conference on Systems Sciences,* Hawaii: IEEE Computer Society Press, 4: 156–62.

CHAPTER 10

Integrating Knowledge with Portfolio Optimization

10.1 INTRODUCTION

The Markowitz mean-variance optimization model (1952) is currently the most popular quantitative approach for building portfolios. As discussed in Chapter 3, in this approach the objective is to minimize the portfolio risk involved in realizing a given return. The coefficients in the model, which are usually estimates computed from historical data, may not be effectively adaptive to day-to-day changes in the securities markets; for this reason and others (see Chapter 3), it is desirable to have a mechanism for incorporating up-to-date knowledge of various sorts into the Markowitz model. This chapter will both examine the way in which knowledge is interpreted by the K-FOLIO system for integration with the Markowitz model and illustrate the potential effects of such integration with an empirical example.

10.2   AN UNENHANCED MARKOWITZ MODEL EXAMPLE

As discussed in Chapter 3, the Markowitz model is a quadratic program (QP) that requires as input a vector of expected security returns $(R_1, \ldots R_n)$ and a matrix of return covariances $\| \sigma_{ij} \|$. A single or multi-index model may be used to facilitate the computation of return and covariance coefficients (Sharpe 1963). The output solution is a vector $(x_1, \ldots x_n)$ of fractions (interpreted as percentages) that represent the relative amounts of each security to be included in the portfolio. The QP model may also be modified to a quadratic version of the goal-programming model, if both the return and the risk levels are pretargeted (Ignizio 1976).

Example 10.1

Suppose \$50,000 is invested in 30 candidate stocks, and the target weekly return R_p for the portfolio is 0.0015. Using data collected for 30 major stocks in Korea from 1981 to 1986, the minimum risk value obtained from the basic Markowitz model is a weekly variance of 2.52 x 10^{-4}. The optimal portfolio percentages are

$X_1 = 0.00$	$X_2 = 0.00$	$X_3 = 2.13\%$
$X_4 = 0.00$	$X_5 = 4.89\%$	$X_6 = 0.00$
$X_7 = 0.00$	$X_8 = 3.11\%$	$X_9 = 7.78\%$
$X_{10} = 3.45\%$	$X_{11} = 0.00$	$X_{12} = 1.71\%$
$X_{13} = 0.00$	$X_{14} = 0.00$	$X_{15} = 12.80\%$
$X_{16} = 2.37\%$	$X_{17} = 0.00$	$X_{18} = 0.00$
$X_{19} = 0.57\%$	$X_{20} = 0.00$	$X_{21} = 8.62\%$
$X_{22} = 7.57\%$	$X_{23} = 0.43\%$	$X_{24} = 38.02\%$
$X_{25} = 0.00$	$X_{26} = 0.00$	$X_{27} = 0.80\%$
$X_{28} = 0.00$	$X_{29} = 0.00$	$X_{30} = 5.65\%$

10.3   THE INTERPRETATION OF KNOWLEDGE

If knowledge and preference factors are to be integrated with the QP model, they must be interpreted in such a way as to be compatible with the structure of that model. The process of integration is graphically depicted in Figure 10.1.

The role of the interpreter is to translate the knowledge and preference system output to feed smoothly into the QP model. In general, knowledge can be incorporated into the basic model by modifying coefficients and augmenting the model with additional constraints. In the K-FOLIO ES, the typical statements used by the interpreter are **AMOUNT, PERCENTAGE,** company name, industry name, **EXCEPT**, and composite **GRADE**s of companies. The company name, industry name, and **EXCEPT** statements determine the decision variables; **GRADE** determines priority on decision variables; and **AMOUNT** and **PERCENTAGE** determine the right-hand-side values of auxiliary constraints.

The following examples will show how knowledge can be transformed into rules.

Example 10.2

RULE	rule 81
CR =	0.7
IF	Company = C_1
OR	Company = C_2
THEN	GRADE = AA
	AMOUNT ≤ 100,000
AND	PERCENTAGE = 10%

The constraints derived from Rule 81 are

$$M(x_1 + x_2) \leq 100,000 \tag{10.1}$$

$$x_1 + x_2 = 0.1, \tag{10.2}$$

where x_1 and x_2 are the fractions of a portfolio held in stocks C_1 and C_2, respectively, and M is the amount of total investment.

Figure 10.1
Integration of Knowledge and Preference Systems with
Quadratic-Programming Model

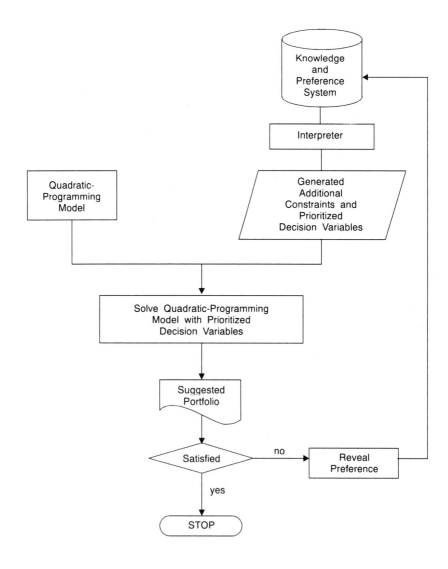

Example 10.3

> RULE   rule 82
> CR =   0.8
> IF   Industry = I_1
> THEN   AMOUNT ≤ 500,000
> OR   PERCENTAGE ≤ 20%
>   EXCEPT C_3, C_4

The constraints derived from Rule 82 are in the following mixed 0-1 integer programming form:

$$M \cdot \sum_{\substack{i \in I_1 \\ i \neq C_3, C_4}} x_i - By_1 \leq 500,000 \tag{10.3}$$

$$\sum_{\substack{i \in I_1 \\ i \neq C_3, C_4}} x_i - By_2 \leq 20\% \tag{10.4}$$

$$y_1 + y_2 \leq 1 \tag{10.5}$$
$$y_1, y_2 = 0, 1 \tag{10.6}$$

where B stands for a very big number.

Example 10.4

> RULE   rule 83
> CR =   0.9
> IF   P/E Ratio ≤ 7
> AND   Annual Sales Growth Rate ≥ 30%
> THEN   AMOUNT = 400,000

In order to interpret Rule 83, it is necessary to identify the companies that satisfy the condition. The derived constraint is

$$M \cdot \sum_{i \in D} x_i = 400{,}000,\tag{10.7}$$

where D is the company set that satisfies the condition of Rule 83.

10.4   QUADRATIC PROGRAMMING WITH PRIORITIZED DECISION VARIABLES

Thus far, these example rules have not mentioned GRADE or credibility. As discussed, information about GRADE and credibility is incorporated into the composite grade for each company in the *composite-grade base*. Since each company has its own unique grade, the notion of grade can be interpreted as being a priority of the decision variables. For instance, the grade *AAA* has top priority, the grade *AA* has the next highest priority, and so on. The modified QP solution process with prioritized decision variables is as follows:

1.   Formulate the original QP model given by (3.1), (3.2), (3.3), (3.4) in Chapter 3. The additional types of constraints described in that chapter could be included as well. Except for the return on portfolio R_p, which is provided by the investor, all coefficients are retrieved from the database.

2.   Add appropriate *derived constraints,* such as the ones in (10.1) through (10.7), to the QP model.

3.   Group the decision variables by their priority level:

Grade	Priority Group
AAA	P_1
AA	P_2
A	P_3
. . .	. . .

4. Set P_1 as the active candidate decision variable group; that is, $P_k = P_1$ and $r_k = 1$ for (10.9 below).

5. Solve the QP model by using the modified objective function (10.8) below, subject to the original Markowitz model constraints (3.2) and (3.4), plus the constraints (10.9), (10.10), and (10.11):

$$\underset{X/i,j\in P_k}{\text{minimize}} \sum_{i=1}^{n} \sum_{j=1}^{n} \sigma_{ij} x_i x_j + s_k \qquad (10.8)$$
$$s_k$$

subject to

$$\sum_{i=1}^{n} R_i x_i = R_p \qquad \{(3.2)\}$$

$$x_i \geq 0, \quad i = 1, \ldots n, \qquad \{(3.4)\}$$

$$\sum_{i \in P_k} x_i + s_k = r_k \qquad (10.9)$$

$$s_k \geq 0 \qquad (10.10)$$

plus the set of *derived constraints*. $\qquad (10.11)$

6. The s_k can be viewed as a slack variable. If $s_k = 0$, the current priority group (including the higher priority groups) can absorb the entire available capital; thus, the solution has been found, so stop.

7. If $s_k > 0$, the current priority group cannot absorb the available capital. Therefore, set $r_{k+1} = s_k$, and select P_{k+1} as the new active candidate decision variable group. Go to step 5.

Example 10.5

From Example 10.1, suppose the expert's knowledge has rated companies C_1, C_9 as *AAA*, C_{12}, C_{27} as *AA*, and so on. In addition, suppose the investor has revealed a preference by the following rules:

RULE   Rule 88

CR =   0.8

IF   Company = C_1

OR   Company = C_3

OR   Company = C_{27}

THEN   GRADE = A

         $0.35 \leq$ PERCENTAGE ≤ 0.5

         BECAUSE . . .

RULE   Rule 89

IF   P/E Ratio ≤ 10

AND   Annual Sales Growth Rate ≥ 50

THEN $10{,}000 \leq$ AMOUNT $\leq 20{,}000$

         (C_9 and C_{27} satisfy Rule 89)

RULE   Rule 90

IF   Company = C_5

OR   Company = C_9

OR   Company = C_{12}

THEN $0.3 \leq$ PERCENTAGE ≤ 0.7

         BECAUSE . . .

Step 1:   Constraint Derivation
The constraints derived from the preference rules are

$$0.35 \leq X_1 + X_3 + X_{27} \leq 0.5$$
$$10{,}000 \leq 50{,}000\,(X_9 + X_{27}) \leq 20{,}000$$
$$0.3 \leq X_5 + X_9 + X_{12} \leq 0.7.$$

Step 2:   The priority levels classified by composite grade are

$$AAA : \quad C_1, C_9$$
$$AA : \quad C_{12}, C_{27}$$

$$A: \quad C_2, C_5, C_{11}, C_{17}, C_{20}, C_{21}$$
$$BBB: \quad C_4, C_6, C_7, C_{13}, C_{24}$$
$$BB: \quad C_8, C_{10}, C_{22}, C_{28}, C_{29}$$
$$B: \quad C_{14}, C_{23}$$
$$CCC: \quad C_{15}, C_{25}$$
$$CC: \quad C_3, C_{16}, C_{19}, C_{26}$$
$$C: \quad C_{18}$$
$$D: \quad C_{30}.$$

Step 3: Initially focus on priority level AAA.

Step 4: The modified constraints for level AAA are

$$0.35 \leq X_1 \leq 0.5$$
$$10,000 \leq 50,000 \, X_9 \leq 20,000$$
$$0.3 \leq X_9 \leq 0.7.$$

Solve the QP with the above additional constraints, which gives the solution

$$X_1 = 35.00\% \qquad X_9 = 35.60\%.$$

The slack s_1 is 0.294, which means that 29.4% of total investment is remaining for further investment in stocks having priority level AA or lower.

Step 5: Set $r_2 = s_1 = 0.293$, and now focusing on priority level AA, repeat Step 4. Keeping in mind that priority AA variables X_{27} and X_{12} must be nonnegative, the additional constraints are

$$0.35 - 0.35 \leq X_{27} \leq 0.5 - 0.35$$
$$\max (0, 10,000 - 50,000 \cdot 0.356) \leq 50,000 \, X_{27} \leq 20,000 - 50,000 \cdot 0.356$$
$$\max (0, 0.3 - 0.356) \leq X_{12} \leq 0.7 - 0.356.$$

The new solution is

$$X_{12} = 29.35\% \qquad X_{27} = 0.05\%.$$

and the final portfolio is

$$X_1 = 35.00\% \qquad X_9 = 35.60\%$$
$$X_{12} = 29.35\% \qquad X_{27} = 0.05\%.$$

Note that this portfolio differs considerably from the one obtained using the unenhanced Markowitz model in Example 10.1.

10.5   PERFORMANCE EVALUATION

To illustrate the potential effects of considering knowledge in portfolio selection, the results of an empirical study using K-FOLIO are summarized in tables 10.1, 10.2, and 10.3 (Lee, Trippi, Chu, and Kim 1990). For the first working day of each month from January through December 1987, Table 10.1 shows actual average market returns (in real time, on a percentage basis); Table 10.2, the realized returns of the unenhanced Markowitz model; and Table 10.3, the realized returns of K-FOLIO's portfolios. Tables 10.2 and 10.3 show actual portfolio returns for expected or target annual returns ranging from 10 percent to 20 percent. The rules were induced from weekly data of 1986.

Table 10.1
Monthly Market Returns

Last Working Day of	Average Return on Market (%)
January	22.538
February	13.147
March	25.474
April	−11.835
May	6.917
June	2.537
July	5.805
August	−6.411
September	−1.445
October	0.809
November	−1.595
December	13.179

Table 10.2
Realized Returns on Markowitz Portfolios

Last Working Day of	Annual Expected Return Target (%)					
	10	**12**	**14**	**16**	**18**	**20**
January	19.128	21.442	23.636	25.280	26.329	30.948
February	33.101	33.044	33.403	33.601	33.720	29.742
March	47.769	39.947	31.859	23.706	19.210	18.572
April	-9.327	-9.549	-9.695	-9.891	-10.163	-9.337
May	6.659	7.601	8.530	9.396	9.499	7.995
June	4.970	4.819	4.733	4.851	4.832	3.356
July	1.972	1.163	0.421	0.021	-0.578	-0.892
August	-4.310	-3.885	-3.524	-3.529	-2.256	1.805
September	-1.752	-1.330	-0.942	-0.852	-0.737	-0.775
October	2.654	3.088	3.495	3.857	3.916	3.447
November	1.829	3.024	4.258	5.341	6.601	6.407
December	9.725	7.768	5.694	3.709	2.127	1.449

Table 10.3
Realized Returns of K-FOLIO Portfolios

Last Working Day of	Annual Expected Return Target (%)					
	10	**12**	**14**	**16**	**18**	**20**
January	28.027	31.339	34.652	37.964	37.532	41.726
February	39.386	38.668	37.950	37.232	34.711	19.897
March	56.886	46.045	35.203	24.361	15.608	14.210
April	-11.080	-12.031	-12.982	-13.933	-13.942	-13.505
May	3.479	5.337	7.195	9.054	8.129	3.789
June	6.019	6.837	7.655	8.473	8.718	6.786
July	-0.350	-1.122	-1.893	-2.665	-3.887	-4.555
August	-2.329	-3.875	-5.421	-6.967	-7.115	-5.218
September	-0.508	-0.867	-1.226	-1.585	-2.440	-3.980
October	3.861	4.363	4.865	5.367	5.120	4.271
November	0.425	1.394	2.364	3.333	3.602	1.019
December	9.879	8.512	7.145	5.779	5.572	8.395

For this static rule set, the incorporation of knowledge by K-FOLIO enables its portfolios to beat the average market return and the unenhanced Markowitz model for the first two months of use. From March 1987 on, however, K-FOLIO's returns are no longer consistently superior to those of the unenhanced Markowitz model. As the anomalies that generated superior returns appear to have a persistence measured in, at most, months, it is important to update the knowledge base fairly frequently.

It is interesting that even without updating, K-FOLIO returns exceed average market returns and unenhanced Markowitz model returns 9 and 8 months out of 12 for the target portfolio return of 10 percent. K-FOLIO returns exceed average market returns only 6 times out of 12 when the target returns are 16%, 18%, and 20%, but the accumulated K-FOLIO returns exceed average market return over the entire year.

It is apparent that the realized return is very sensitive to the target return R_p; thus, the choice of this parameter is important to the performance of the system. Figures 10.2 and 10.3 plot the realized returns vs. time for targets of 12% and 18%.

Figure 10.2
Realized Returns; 12% Target

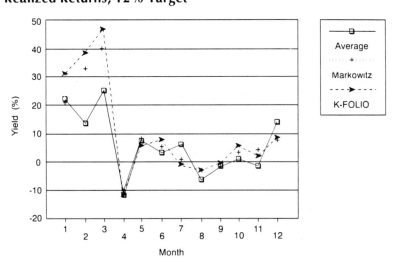

Figure 10.3
Realized Returns; 18% Target

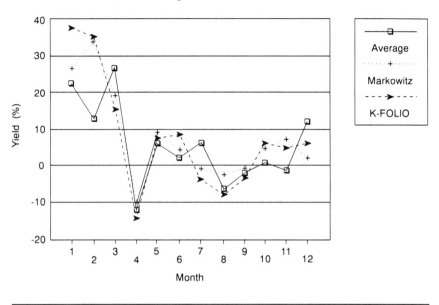

10.6   SUMMARY

Knowledge can be interpreted as priorities and constraints in the Markowitz model. In an illustrative empirical study, it was shown that integrating knowledge with the Markowitz model can significantly improve the model's performance; thus knowledge can be beneficially used in making portfolio selection decisions as well as in evaluating and explaining individual stocks.

REFERENCES

Ignizio, J. P., 1976. *Programming and Extensions.* Lexington Books.

Lee, J. K., Trippi, R. R., Chu, S. C., and Kim, H. S., 1990. K-FOLIO: Integrating the Markowitz Model with a Knowledge-based System. *Journal of Portfolio Management* 17 (Fall): 89–93.

Markowitz, H., 1952. Portfolio Selec tion. *The Journal of Finance* 7 (March): 77–91.

Sharpe, W. F. A Simplified Model for Portfolio Analysis. *Management Science* 9 (January): 277–93.

CHAPTER 11

Integrating Knowledge with Databases

11.1   INTRODUCTION

In Section 6.3, the role of databases in portfolio decision making was introduced. This chapter will review in more detail the components of databases that support investment decisions; identify the distinguishing characteristics of relational, object-oriented, and knowledge bases; discuss the management of financial data and price and trading-volume data; and examine the methods by which the capabilities of databases can be extended through the use of predefined functions.

11.2   DATABASE EVOLUTION

As database technology has evolved, so has its terminology. This chapter will examine the databases popularly referred to as *relational databases, object-oriented databases,* and *knowledge bases.*

11.2.1   Relational Databases

The terms *database* and *knowledge base* are both widely used in the information systems field. Although the two terms have arisen independently, the software systems they refer to are basically similar.

In the 1970s, products were developed that supported the storage of information in table-like *databases,* or *relational databases* that had formats such as that shown in Figure 11.1. Earlier storage structures had been mainly of the hierarchical and network types. Database administrators' major concerns at this time were to remove redundancy in corporate databases; determine the efficiency of *relational algebras* for retrieving, updating, and joining data having multiple relations; and find a type of *relational calculus* that could represent information for retrieval without ambiguity (see Date 1986).

In the early days of computer information systems, databases were used to facilitate corporate-level data sharing, and consisted of large-scale mainframes attached to a number of terminals. The first databases to handle stock-price and trading-volume data were generally of this type. As a result of the widespread availability of microcomputers and electronic data sources during the 1980s, investment databases began to include personal computer DBMSs (data base management systems); thus downloading of a local or remote mainframe's database to the PC database and the management of distributed databases have become im-

Figure 11.1
Example of Relational Format

Stock Name	Price	Trading Volume	Date	
Slick Oil Co	99 1/2	22,500	3/10/92	
Junk Food Co	15 1/4	9,200	3/10/92	
MBT Electric	28	65,000	3/10/92	
Bank East	12 3/8	7,500	3/10/92	
Go Motor Corp	52	88,300	3/10/92	
Fast Computer	12 5/8	25,000	3/10/92	
Slick Oil Co	98 3/4	18,000	3/11/92	
Junk Food Co	15 1/2	11,700	3/11/92	
•	•	•	•	
•	•	•	•	
•	•	•	•	

portant concerns for users of investment databases and on-line data services. Some common DBMSs are DB2, INGRES, ORACLE, dBASE IV, and FoxBase.

11.2.2   The Advent of Knowledge Bases

In the 1980s, many in the expert system community referred to their databases as *knowledge bases*. In the earliest versions of rule-based shells, the knowledge base was divided into a rule base and a fact base (sometimes called working memory). In most systems, the role of a fact base is exactly the same as that of a traditional database. Because of this, in the ES world the fact base is sometimes called a database.

In early ESs, fact bases were simply lists. These were very inefficient for the retrieval and modification of data. Today it is possible to interface a relational database with an ES's fact base, or to replace the fact base entirely with a relational database (or with something else). Most of the commercially successful ES shells interface with popular databases such as dBASE IV and with spreadsheets, rather than using these products for primary data storage.

Workstation-level tools such as KEE, ART, Knowledge Craft, and Nexpert Object support frame-based knowledge representation as well as rule-based representation. In these hybrid tools, the fact base can take the form of a frame base, such as that described in Section 5.3. Also, in most of these products the relational database is not absorbed into the expert system, just interfaced. In the 1990s, such frame-based ES tools as Kappa, ART-IM, and Nexpert Object migrated from workstations to personal computers.

11.2.3   Object-oriented Databases

To most knowledge engineers, a relational database is just another means of storing knowledge. To database developers, a knowledge base is nothing more than a sophisticated database. As a result, terms such as *deductive database* and *object-oriented database* have emerged. As illustrated in the Prolog language example (see Figure 11.2), a deductive database adds rules on top of an existing database. Any rule-based system can be considered a deductive database if one focuses on its database. Which function is viewed as major and which is viewed as supplementary is a matter of perspective. Currently, it is common for the term object-oriented database to be used interchangeably with the term frame-based knowledge base. In order to be consistent with popular usage, these will also be referred to as object-oriented databases.

Figure 11.2
Illustrative Facts and Rules in Prolog

```
horizon (short_term)
risk_attitude (adverse)
dollar (strong)
labor_relations (bad)
inflation (high)
gulf_crisis (last_short)

use (machine_learned_knowledge) if horizon (short_term)
recession (end) if gulf_crisis (last_short)
```

11.3   THE MANAGEMENT OF FINANCIAL DATA

This section will examine the data-management issues that arise among investors. Naturally, one data type of universal interest to this group is financial (including ratio) data.

11.3.1   The Organization of Financial Data

Accounting and other publicly available financial data are usually updated quarterly or annually. Since both expert systems and other reporting systems make use of financial data on individual stocks, companies, and industries, it is necessary to maintain this data in both object-oriented and relational databases. For stocks, data on average price, average trading volume, price-earning ratio, and beta will be needed. For companies, data must be kept on sales, sales growth rate, amount of exports, debt ratio, fixed ratio, major products, assets, and profits as a percentage of sales, equity and so on. For industries, data on average price index, total trading volume, total sales, sales growth rate, amount of exports, profitability, tax advantages, and stage in life cycle must be maintained.

Inheritance from higher to lower level and average-up or sum-up from lower to higher level are effective ways of handling the class-instance relationships of stocks, companies, and industries. For example, industry-level tax benefits can be inherited by companies in the industry, while the sum of sales, sales growth and amount of exports can summed up from companies to industries. The price and trading volume of stocks can also be averaged up to both companies and industry levels.

As illustrated in Figure 11.3, in which direct input, sum-up, and average-up mechanisms are shown, the object-oriented database can be highly effective for representing such relationships. Since such data is also necessary for other reports, a relational database will normally have to be maintained in parallel for the same data (see Figure 11.4). As data is usually received first into the relational database, a facility is required to make the transformation into the object-oriented database. The inheritance and average-up/sum-up facility will probably not exist in the relational database, so specific programs will have to be written in the host language in order to derive the necessary data items.

Figure 11.3
Object-oriented Database

{{Industry
    AVERAGE PRICE INDEX : *average-up from stocks*
    TOTAL TRADING VOLUME : *sum-up from stocks*
    TOTAL SALES : *sum-up from company*
    SALES GROWTH RATE : *average-up from company*
    AMOUNT OF EXPORTS : *sum-up from company*
    PROFIT (%) : *average-up from company*
    TAX BENEFIT : *direct input*
    STAGE IN LIFE CYCLE : *direct input*}}

{{Company
    SALES : *direct input*
    SALES GROWTH RATE : *direct input*
    AMOUNT OF EXPORT : *direct input*
    DEBT RATIO : *direct input*
    FIXED RATIO : *direct input*
    MAJOR PRODUCTS : *direct input*
    ASSETS : *direct input*
    PROFITS (%) : *direct input*
    TAX BENEFIT : *inherit from industry*
    AVERAGE PRICE : *average-up from stocks*
    AVERAGE TRADING VOLUME : *average-up from stocks*
    PRICE-EARNING RATIO : *average-up from stocks*
    BETA : *average-up from stocks*}}

{{Stock
    AVERAGE PRICE : *direct input*
    AVERAGE TRADING VOLUME : *direct input*
    PRICE-EARNING RATIO : *direct input*
    BETA : *direct input*
    SALES : *inherit from company*
    SALES GROWTH RATE : *inherit from company*
    AMOUNT OF EXPORT : *inherit from company*
    DEBT RATIO : *inherit from company*
    FIXED RATIO : *inherit from company*
    MAJOR PRODUCTS : *inherit from company*
    ASSETS : *inherit from company*
    PROFITS (%) : *inherit from company*
    TAX BENEFIT : *inherit from company*}}

Figure 11.4
Relational Database

Industry

Industry	Tax Benefit	Stage in Life Cycle

Company

Company	Sales	Sales Growth Rate	Amount of Export	Debt Ratio	Fixed Ratio	Major Product	Assets	Profit

Stock

Stock	Average Price	Average Trading Volume

11.3.2   The Use of Financial Data

Currently available financial data can be sent through either interactive retrieval or matching with rules. In K-FOLIO, financial data may be retrieved during stock-evaluation dialogues (see Section 6.5). Financial data may also be matched with the rule set in order to identify relevant rules for each stock. (See the inference procedure described in Section 6.4.)

Through the use of inductive learning mechanisms (see Chapter 9), historical financial series can be used to generate rules for long-term fundamental analysis. Since these data are usually updated quarterly or annually, a machine-learned rule may last for three or six months; thus, it is not necessary to update or match such rules over fairly long time intervals.

11.4   THE MANAGEMENT OF PRICE AND TRADING-VOLUME DATA

11.4.1   The Organization of Price and Volume Data

Price and trading volume data should be updated at least daily; these data are frequently displayed in graphs showing stock-price trend lines, moving-average curves of stock prices, moving-average curves of trading volume, and price-volume correlation curves (see Figure 9.4 through 9.7). One reason for displaying current price and trading volume dynamically in graphical form is to make it easier to interpret suspected price anomalies. For example, in Section 9.4 it was shown how the SYNPLE algorithm can generate credible pattern-based rules from such data. The quantity of data to be saved varies; if moving averages are rule inputs, then quantity will be determined by the interval of the longest moving average. As new data enters, old data can be dropped.

In order to uncover any anomalies that may involve both trading and fundamental data, and generate corresponding rules, it is desirable to keep historical daily data for years. Since pattern-based inductive learning takes a significant amount of computing time, one would probably want to use a dedicated personal computer or workstation for this purpose. Once rules are generated, the rule file can be transferred to the operating computer.

If charts showing daily price and trading volume are to be displayed, recent daily data must be kept in the object-oriented database. Since price and volume data are usually obtained from the mainframes of security companies or from independent on-line data services, at least one download daily to the expert-system-serving workstation will be needed. It is common for data to be downloaded continuously, with a signal given when a desired action is triggered.

11.4.2   The Uses of Price and Volume Data

Daily price and trading-volume-based rules are usually used for short-term trading, but if the interval of data collection is expanded for weekly and monthly averaging, this data can also be used for investment strategies that employ long-term data.

11.5   MANAGEMENT OF THE FUNCTION BASE

If only the data items in the database are to be utilized, the attributes of rules should be limited to such items. This is a fairly strict restriction, so the scope of rule statements could be severely limited. To overcome such a limitation, one can utilize *functions* incorporating *reserved words.*

11.5.1   Functions

Suppose that the database includes *net profit growth rate* and *sales growth rate,* and that the attribute to be included in a rule is the ratio of net profit growth to sales growth. This can be accomplished by defining the following function:

ratio of net profit growth to sales growth

= net profit growth rate / sales growth rate

The function base includes a collection of such functions that can operate on the data items in the database. This approach extends the boundary of data items greatly, without adding significantly to the storage burden.

In order to facilitate the creation of required functions, the inference engine needs to identify attributes that do not currently exist in either the database attributes list or in the function base. The user can then define additional functions, assuming the necessary attributes can be derived from the existing data items. If the derivation is not possible, either that attribute in the rule base should be avoided or the attribute should be added to the database items.

11.5.2   Reserved Words

In addition to functions, and in order to allow compact expressions in rule specifications, K-FOLIO also supports the following reserved works associated with stock price and trading volume: SIGMA, MAX, MIN, WHENMAX, WHENMIN, and SELECT. The following are some examples of how these reserved words may be used for a certain stock:

SIGMA(VOLUME, 040192, –30): Sum of trading volumes for 30 days previous to April 1, 1992

MAX(PRICE, 040192, 10): Maximum stock price for 10 days after April 1, 1992

MIN(PRICE, 040192, –10): Minimum stock price for 10 days previous to April 1, 1992

WHENMAX(VOLUME, 040192, 20): The date with the highest trading volume among the 20 days following April 1, 1992

WHENMIN(PRICE, 040192, –20): The date with the minimum stock price among the 20 days previous to April 1, 1992.

SELECT(PRICE, 040192): The stock price on April 1, 1992

By combining functions with reserved words, more complex functions can be defined, as in the following examples:

SIGMA(PRICE, today, –30)/30: 30 days moving average of stock price

SELECT(PRICE, WHENMAX(VOLUME, 040192, 10)): The stock price on the day with the maximum trading volume during the 10 days following April 1, 1992

The values derivable by functions and reserved works can also be retrieved as though they were items defined in the database.

11.6   SUMMARY AND CONCLUSIONS

It is important to incorporate the knowledge base with security, company, and industry databases. Relational databases, object-oriented databases, and knowledge bases can all be used for portfolio decision support in ESs. The theoretical distinction between data and knowledge is vague and sometimes arbitrary, and the conventional relational databases that store financial data, stock prices, and trading volumes are used not only by the ES but also by other reporting systems. Generally, then, it is best to loosely couple the relational database with the object-oriented database (Jarke and Vassiliou 1983). Maintaining consistency between a corporate and/or investor level relational database and a localized object-oriented database should be a key part of investment data management.

REFERENCES

Date, C. J., 1986. *An Introduction to Database Systems,* 4th ed., 1. Addison Wesley Publishing Company.

Jarke, M., and Vassiliou, Y., 1983. Coupling Expert Systems with Database Management, *Artificial Intelligence Applications for Business,* ed. W. Reitman. Proceedings of the NYU Symposium, 65–86.

CHAPTER 12

An Illustrative
Session with K-FOLIO

12.1   INTRODUCTION

By describing a typical dialogue session with K-FOLIO, this chapter will illustrate many of the concepts discussed in this book. The dialogues are arranged as follows: selection of investment characteristics, environmental assumptions, and knowledge sources; individual stock or industry evaluation; criteria-based evaluation; grade-based listing; and portfolio selection. The version of K-FOLIO used for the dialogue examples was implemented at the Seoul-based Lucky Securities Company.

The system, called BRAINS, runs on an IBM-compatible personal computer under the MS-DOS operating system.

12.2   SELECTING INVESTMENT CHARACTERISTICS, ENVIRONMENTAL ASSUMPTIONS, AND KNOWLEDGE SOURCES

Since investment characteristics and environmental assumptions determine the selection of relevant knowledge, the dialogue begins with the selection of characteristics and assumptions. As shown in Figure 12.1, investment characteristics may be defined by selecting an investment horizon and a risk attitude. The investment horizon is to call up relevant knowledge and to determine the evaluation time lag in the machine-learning scheme (see Section 9.3) and the risk attitude query is used to select the target return for the Markowitz model.

A binary selection of assumptions (Y or N) is illustrated in Figure 12.2. In this example, the environmental factors are the strength of the dollar, the recession, labor relations, inflation, and the duration of a political Persian Gulf Crisis. Because binary selection of assumptions is a

Figure 12.1
Selection of Investment Characteristics

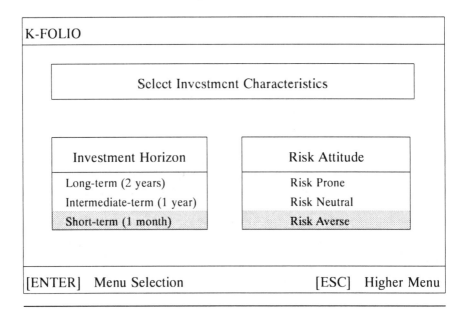

Figure 12.2
Selection of Assumptions

K-FOLIO		
	Select Assumptions	
	Assumptions	ANSWER (Y/N)
	Strong Dollar	Y
	Recession Continues	N
	Poor Labor Relations Outlook	Y
	High Inflation	N
	Gulf Crisis Lasts Short	Y
[ENTER] Menu Selection		[ESC] Higher Menu

relatively crude facility, fuzzy membership values could be assigned to factors for which binary selections are difficult to make.

As shown in Figure 12.3, the last of the preliminary steps is to select a knowledge base. In this example, the expert knowledge base (see Section 6.2) and machine-learned knowledge base (see Chapter 9) are selected. After completing the dialogues shown in Figures 12.1 through 12.3, the user is ready to select the options shown in Figure 12.4.

12.3   INDIVIDUAL STOCK EVALUATION

In order to initiate stock evaluation, the user can select Option 1 from those given in Figure 12.4. The display will then show candidate stocks and enable the user to select an individual stock (see Figure 12.5). In this case, stock ABC has been selected, and the screen shown in Figure 12.6 appears. This screen shows a composite grade BBB and ordered

Figure 12.3
Selection of Knowledge Bases

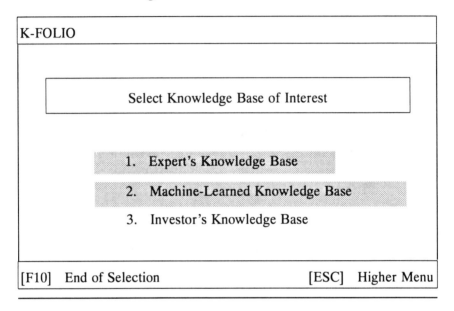

reasons by the grade level. If the user cannot agree with the elementary grades and credibilities in the Reasons section, he or she can modify them interactively. As shown in Figure 12.7, the grade and credibility of Reason 3 are modified to the values A and 1.0, and the composite grade is recomputed to the value A (see Figure 12.8). Note that the order of reasons is also rearranged.

12.4   INDUSTRY EVALUATION

In order to initiate industry evaluation, the user selects Option 2 in Figure 12.4, which brings up the screen shown in Figure 12.9. If, for example, industry "An_Industry" is selected, the industry evaluation screen shown in figure 12.10 will be displayed. Interactive dialogue is supported for both industry and individual stock evaluation (see Figures 12.7 and 12.8).

Figure 12.4
Dialogue Menu

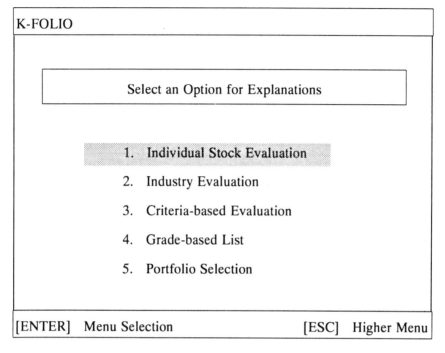

12.5   CRITERIA-BASED DIALOGUE

In order to evaluate the stocks that satisfy a certain set of criteria (see Section 6.5.3), the user can select the desired criteria from the menu shown in Figure 12.11. In this case, debt ratio is selected as the first criterion. If the user selects operator "<" and types in *300*, the statement *debt ratio < 300* will be generated (see Figure 12.12). If a criterion (e.g., industry) has predefined multiple choices, the candidate values will be displayed (see Figure 12.13). The user is then shown the average grade of the stocks that satisfy the criteria, along with a list of the stocks (see Figure 12.14).

Figure 12.5
Selection of Individual Stocks

K-FOLIO		Individual Stock: Short-term

Select a Stock

ABC	Aetna Life & Casualty	Alcan Aluminum Ltd.
Amax. Inc.	Amerada Hess Corp.	American Home Products
AT&T	Anheuser-Busch, Inc.	Atlantic Richfield
Campbell Soup Co.	Carnation Co.	CBS, Inc.
Chase Manhattan Co.	Coca-Cola Co.	Conoco, Inc.
Digital Equipment Co.	Dow Chemical Co.	Emerson Electric
Exxon Corp.	Federated Dept. Store	Florida Power & Light
Foster Wheeler Co.	Gannett, Inc.	General Electric
General Motors	Georgia-Pacific	Gulf Oil Corp.
INA Corp.	Ingersoll Rand	IBM
Johnson & Johnson	Koppers, Inc.	Kroger Co.
Lone Star Industries	R. H. Macy & Co., Inc.	Maytag Co.
McDonald's Corp.	Medtronic, Inc.	Melville Corp.
Merck & Co., Inc.	Midland Ross Corp.	Minnesota M & M
Monsanto Co.	Motorola, Inc.	NCNB Corp.

[ENTER]   Menu Selection   [ESC]   Higher Menu

12.6   GRADE-BASED LISTING

The grade-based list of stocks is obtained by selecting Menu Item 4 from the screen shown in Figure 12.4. The new screen is shown in Figure 12.15.

Figure 12.6
Grade and Reasons for Individual Stock

```
┌────────────────────────────────────────────────────────────────┐
│ K-FOLIO                          Individual Stock:   Short-term │
│                                                                  │
│    Grade of ABC = BBB                                            │
│                                                                  │
│    Reasons:                                                      │
│                                                                  │
│    (1)   Grade = AA with CR = 0.8                                │
│          The electronic industry that the company ABC belongs to │
│          is a high-growth industry.                             │
│    (2)   Grade = BBB with CR = 0.8                               │
│          Reserved Ratio > 200                                    │
│    (3)   Grade = BB with CR = 0.9                                │
│          Sales Growth Rate ≥ 20%                                 │
│                                                                  │
│                                                                  │
└────────────────────────────────────────────────────────────────┘
```

[F4 Graph]   [F5 Timing]   [ENTER Continue]   [ESC Higher Menu]

12.7 PORTFOLIO SELECTION

In order to construct a portfolio by using the knowledge-augmented Markowitz optimization model, the user selects Menu Item 5 from the display (see Figure 12.4). The interpreter (see Section 10.3) is then invoked. In formulating the optimization model, the investment amount and average annual expected return are input (see Figure 12.16); the user then chooses one of two possible strategies for applying the knowledge: *composite-grade*-based order or *degree-of-underestimation*-based order (see Figure 12.17). The composite-grade-based order strategy applies grades as the preemptive priority; thus, stocks with *AAA* will be selected first; stocks with *AA* will be selected second; and so on. The degree-of-underestimation ordering strategy categorizes stocks according to the magnitude of the difference between the realized stock-price level

Figure 12.7
On-Screen Edit

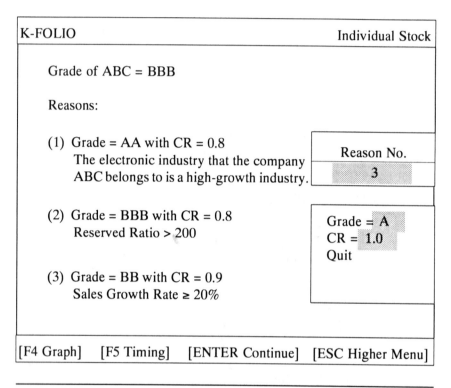

| K-FOLIO | Individual Stock |

Grade of ABC = BBB

Reasons:

(1) Grade = AA with CR = 0.8
The electronic industry that the company
ABC belongs to is a high-growth industry.

Reason No.
3

(2) Grade = BBB with CR = 0.8
Reserved Ratio > 200

Grade = A
CR = 1.0
Quit

(3) Grade = BB with CR = 0.9
Sales Growth Rate ≥ 20%

[F4 Graph]   [F5 Timing]   [ENTER Continue]   [ESC Higher Menu]

and the computed grade. If a stock is highly undergraded, it is considered to have good appreciation potential.

If the composite-grade-based strategy is selected, a trial portfolio is returned (see Figure 12.18). The difference between the current portfolio and suggested trial portfolio defines the trades that should be executed. If the user has no objection, the dialogue can be terminated; if the user wishes to modify the suggested portfolio, some stocks can be eliminated and others can be added on. Stocks to be eliminated are selected from the list shown in Figure 12.19. The grade of such stocks is treated as ZZZ in the investor preference base (see Chapter 8), which implies a grade of *D* irrespective of the grades of the other factors (see Section 6.4.2). On the other hand, the newly added stocks are treated as "***", which implies a grade of AAA irrespective of the grades of other fac-

Figure 12.8
Modified Screen after Revision

```
┌──────────────────────────────────────────────────────────────┐
│ K-FOLIO                        Individual Stock:   Short-term  │
├──────────────────────────────────────────────────────────────┤
│                                                                │
│    Grade of ABC = A                                            │
│                                                                │
│    Reasons:                                                    │
│                                                                │
│    (1)  Grade = AA with CR = 0.8                               │
│         The electronic industry that the company ABC belongs to│
│         is a high-growth industry.                             │
│                                                                │
│    (2)  Grade = A with CR = 1.0                                │
│         Sales Growth Rate ≥ 20%                                │
│                                                                │
│    (3)  Grade = BBB with CR = 0.8                              │
│         Reserved Ratio > 200                                   │
│                                                                │
│                                                                │
│                                                                │
├──────────────────────────────────────────────────────────────┤
│ [F4 Graph]    [F5 Timing]    [ENTER Continue]   [ESC Higher Menu]│
└──────────────────────────────────────────────────────────────┘
```

tors. With the internal revision of these grades, the modified optimization model is rerun to generate a new portfolio. The user can then again initiate the evaluation of individual stocks (see Section 12.3).

12.8   SUMMARY

The example session described in this chapter shows how the K-FOLIO system can implement the concepts described in earlier chapters. At the beginning of the dialogue, K-FOLIO requests investment characteristics (time horizon and risk attitude), environmental assumptions, and knowledge sources (expert, machine-learned, or investor); relevant knowledge bases are then selected. At this point a user can acquire evaluations of industries and individual stocks and generate a set of criteria-satisfying stocks. After the knowledge base is merged with the optimization model, a portfolio can be generated.

Figure 12.9
Selection of Industry

K-FOLIO	Industry: Long-term

Select an Industry

Aerospace	Agriculture and food
Air transport	Apparel
Banks	Business machines
Business services	Chemicals
Construction	Consumer durables
Containers	Domestic oil
Drugs and medicine	Electronics
Energy raw materials	Energy utilities
Forest products and paper	Gold mining and securities
Insurance	International oil
Liquor	Media
Miscellaneous and conglomerates	Miscellaneous finance
Motor vehicles	Nondurables and entertainment
Nonferrous metals	Photographic and optical
Producer goods	Railroads and shipping

[F4 Graph]   [F5 Timing]   [ENTER Continue]   [ESC Higher Menu]

Figure 12.10
Grade and Reason for an Industry

K-FOLIO	Industry

Grade of An_Industry = AA

Reasons:

(1) Grade = A with CR = 0.9
     High-Growth Industry

(2) Grade = AAA with CR = 0.8
     Technologically Competitive Against Japanese Companies

[F4 Graph]   [F5 Timing]   [ENTER Continue]   [ESC Higher Menu]

Figure 12.11
Selection of Criteria

K-FOLIO	Criteria

Select Criteria

Accum. Debt to Fixed Assets	Assets Turnover
Borrowing & Bonds Payable Ratio	Current Ratio
Debt Ratio	Depreciation Ratio
Equity Growth	Equity Ratio
Equity Turnover	Financial Exp. to Borrowings
Financial Exp. to Sales	Fixed Assets Growth
Fixed Assets to Equity & Liabil.	Fixed Assets Turnover
Gross Margin on Sales	Gross Value Added Growth
Industry	Net FX Gains to Sales
Net Income Growth	Ordinary Income on Sales
Ordinary Income on Total Assets	R&D to Sales
Receivables Turnover	Return on Capital Stock
Return on Equity	Return on Sales

[ESC Quit]

Figure 12.12
Numeric-type Criteria Specification

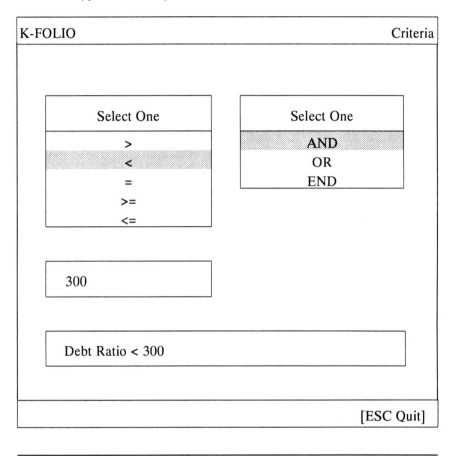

Figure 12.13
Value-type Criteria Specification

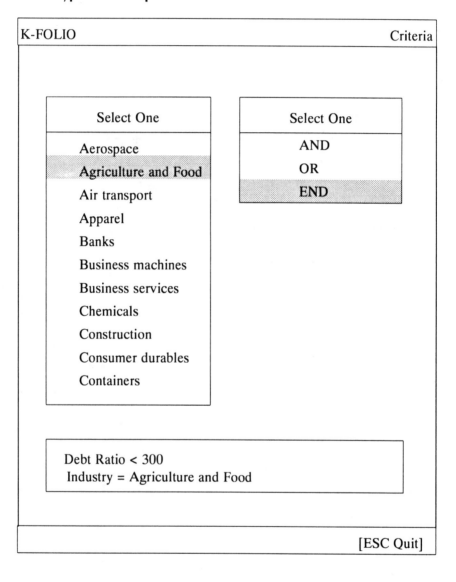

Figure 12.14
Output from Criteria-based Dialogue

K-FOLIO		Criteria
Stock	Debt Ratio	Industry
AF1	153.99	Agriculture and Food
AF2	161.20	Agriculture and Food
AF3	186.05	Agriculture and Food
		[ESC Quit]

Figure 12.15
Grade-based List

K-FOLIO		Grade
(1) AAA :	AAA1 AAA2 AAA3 AAA4 AAA5 AAA6 AAA7 AAA8 AAA9 AAA10	
(2) AA :	AA1 AA2 AA3 AA4 AA5 AA6 AA7 AA8 AA9 AA10 AA11 AA12	
[F4 Previous]	[F5 Next]	[F6 Enter]

Figure 12.16
Input of Investment Amount and Expected Return Target

K-FOLIO	Portfolio

Investment Amount (U.S. $) = 1,000,000

Expected Annual Return (%) = 12

[ESC Quit]

Figure 12.17
Selection of Knowledge-Application Strategy

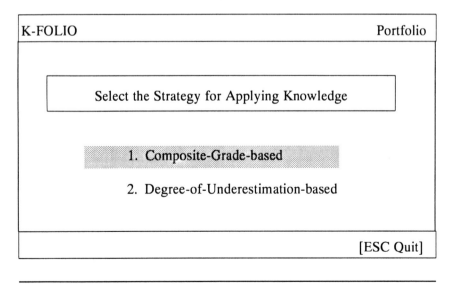

K-FOLIO	Portfolio

Select the Strategy for Applying Knowledge

1. Composite-Grade-based

2. Degree-of-Underestimation-based

[ESC Quit]

Figure 12.18
Trial Portfolio

K-FOLIO				Portfolio

Investment Amount (U.S. $) = 1,000,000
Expected Annual Return (%) = 12
Risk of Portfolio = Low (Standard Deviation = 0.8884)

Portfolio

Stock	Percentage	Amount	Stock Price	Volume
ABM	18.3	183,000	57 1/2	32,300
MLC	11.7	117,000	18 3/8	117,600
PNZ	6.8	68,000	22 1/8	88,400
ASQ	15.5	155,000	86 3/4	135,700
UGE	8.3	83,000	14 5/8	67,100
LRS	6.9	69,000	40 1/4	42,000
BLG	10.1	101,000	65	99,500
RAT	22.4	224,000	47 3/4	144,800
	100.0%	$1,000,000		

[F1 DOS]   [F3 Modify Portfolio]   [ESC Higher Menu]

Figure 12.19
Elimination of Unfavorable Stocks

K-FOLIO	Portfolio

Select stocks to be eliminated

ABM	MLC	PNZ	ASQ	UGE	LRS
BLG	RAT				

[ESC Quit]

REFERENCES

1990. *K-FOLIO User's Manual.* KAIST.

CHAPTER 13

Concluding Remarks

13.1 System-Design Criteria: A Summary
13.2 Directions for Future Research

13.1 SYSTEM-DESIGN CRITERIA: A SUMMARY

This book has covered many aspects of building and using knowledge-based systems for investment decision making. The key system-design issues can be summarized as follows:

1   Rules provide an effective way to represent knowledge in the security-investment domain. The rule-based paradigm can efficiently generate evaluations of securities and industries as well as the reasons leading to those evaluations. Each rule should incorporate a credibility measure and such meta-knowledge as usage, investment horizon, author, entry date, and expiration date. Meta-knowledge facilitates knowledge acquisition and maintenance tasks.

2. For portfolio decisions, a frame-based system is an ideal form of object-oriented database; it provides inheritance, average-up, and sum-up facilities, which are useful for linking securities, industries,

and asset classes. In order to extend the scope of usable data items, virtual data items can be defined by using a function definition language that specifies new items derived from extant data attributes. A loosely coupled relational database will, however, be necessary to support other reports and on-line queries for information irrelevant to the expert system.

3. Inference for investment decisions requires a structured organization of the information acquired from diverse sources for individual securities or industries, plus a means of resolving possibly conflicting evidence into simple composite grades. The organized information can be used to explain the reasons for particular conclusions. If the end user does not agree with the reasons, he or she should be able to modify them and observe the impact of the modification without corrupting the common shared-knowledge base.

4. Representation schemes should be selected by considering the availability of data as well as the performance of associated approximate reasoning mechanisms. The Bayesian, certainty-factor, and fuzzy-logic approaches are all useful for handling investment uncertainties. Nonmonotonic reasoning can also be used to reflect a user's assumptions about the investment environment.

5. If possible, machine-learning techniques should be applied to overcome the bottleneck of knowledge acquisition. For knowledge relevant to long-term investment, ID3 or other inductive means can be used to derive rules based on financial data. For knowledge relevant to short-term trading, pattern-based syntactic learning schemes can be used to generate credible rules automatically from price and trading-volume data. Such schemes can also be used for long-term investment decisions if the relevant rules involve weekly or monthly data points. Genetic algorithms could also be useful for generating synergistic rule sets, and neural networks are a promising medium for detecting pockets of market inefficiency. Nevertheless, since all machine-learning schemes are based on extrapolation, human knowledge is still necessary to assess the likely impact of nonrecurrent events.

6. Optimization models such as the modified Markowitz model (see Chapter 10) can be used to apply reasoning capability to portfolio-mix decisions. The main issues are those associated with accommodating up-to-date knowledge and preferences within the selected

model. This book has shown how grades of stocks can be treated as priorities on decision variables, and how investor-provided restrictions can be treated as additional constraints. In experiments, the knowledge-enhanced optimization model has outperformed both a market index and the unenhanced Markowitz model.

13.2   DIRECTIONS FOR FUTURE RESEARCH

The following issues related to the effectiveness and economy of knowledge-based systems for portfolio management merit further study:

1. The performance of expert systems can be improved by generating more reliable knowledge via machine learning; thus, more attention should be given to developing learning techniques that will be effective in this particular domain. It would be helpful as well to have a framework for synergistically combining such approaches as neural networks, syntactic pattern-based learning, genetic adaptive algorithms, and case-based learning and reasoning schemes. Intensive comparative experiments should accompany the development of any new techniques.

2. More effective synthesis of predictive capability with explanation capability is highly desirable. For example, although clear and concise explanation of reasons is usually essential to investors, neural network-like models do not often provide theoretically acceptable reasons for their recommendations. It is possible, however, that simple probabilities of success will suffice for some types of users, regardless of the reasoning.

3. Incorporating the entire spectrum of concepts and techniques discussed in this book into a single system may be inappropriate, impractical, or too costly for many prospective users. An economical solution to this problem would be to develop a system generator capable of generating specific portfolio investment systems that satisfy a set of specifications given by the potential user.

Index